More Bygone Bridgwater and the Villages

Rod Fitzhugh & Will Loudon

AVALON PRESS, COVENTRY
Coventry, 1989

THE AUTHORS

ROD FITZHUGH, a Legal Adviser with Coventry City Magistrates Court, was born on the Bristol Road in Bridgwater in a house overlooking the River Parrett, and where he lived for his first thirty years, before moving to the Midlands, where he met his wife Celia, a Coventry solicitor. Rod started collecting old postcards of Bridgwater and the area some eight years ago, his friendship with co-author Will Loudon dating from that time. A frequent visitor to Bridgwater, Rod and his wife now have a flat overlooking the docks, where they spend their weekends and holidays, making it easier for them to continue research in readiness for the next book.....

WILL LOUDON came to Bridgwater when only a three years old, is employed with Courtaulds Research, Bridgwater, and has been collecting postcards for about ten years. Will and Jane have three children, and he is a Special Constable with the Somerset and Avon Police Force.

Rod and Will's common interest resulted in publication of *Bygone Bridgwater and the Villages* compiled from their joint collections, this sequel comprising postcards not used then, and new ones found since. The advertisements reproduced have been taken from contemporary literature of the period.

Cover drawn and designed by Rod Fitzhugh
Illustrations from the authors' collections
Printed by Warwick Printing Co. Ltd., Theatre Street, Warwick

ISBN 0 9512774 1 3

More Bygone Bridgwater and the Villages

Bridgwater Photographers, Publishers and Printers

Walter Belcher	29, Fore Street
Bigwood & Staple	6 & 8, York Buildings
C.H. Burrows	4, Hamp Ward
G. Comer	35, Eastover
Coombes & Dilks	68, Eastover
H. Montague-Cooper	38, Wembdon Road
W. Crocker	60, High Street
G.C. Fisher	36, Fore Street
J.C. Hosier	34, Wembdon Road
F.H. Light	6, Cornhill
H.P. Matthews	7, Melbourne Square
Moulton & Paine	10, Penel Orlieu
Osborne & Fisher	20, Cornhill
Page & Son	42, Fore Street
J.H. Phillips	99, St. John Street
W.V. Roberts	29, Eastover
F. Sanders	32, Eastover
Job Slocombe	Valetta Place
W.H. Smith & Son	4, Eastover
Squibbs & Carey	38, Fore Street
C. Temblett	29, Eastover
John Vearncombe	29, Penel Orlieu
The Wessex Studio	46, Camden Road
J. Whitby & Sons Ltd	10, Cornhill
Wood & Son	19, Cornhill

CONTENTS

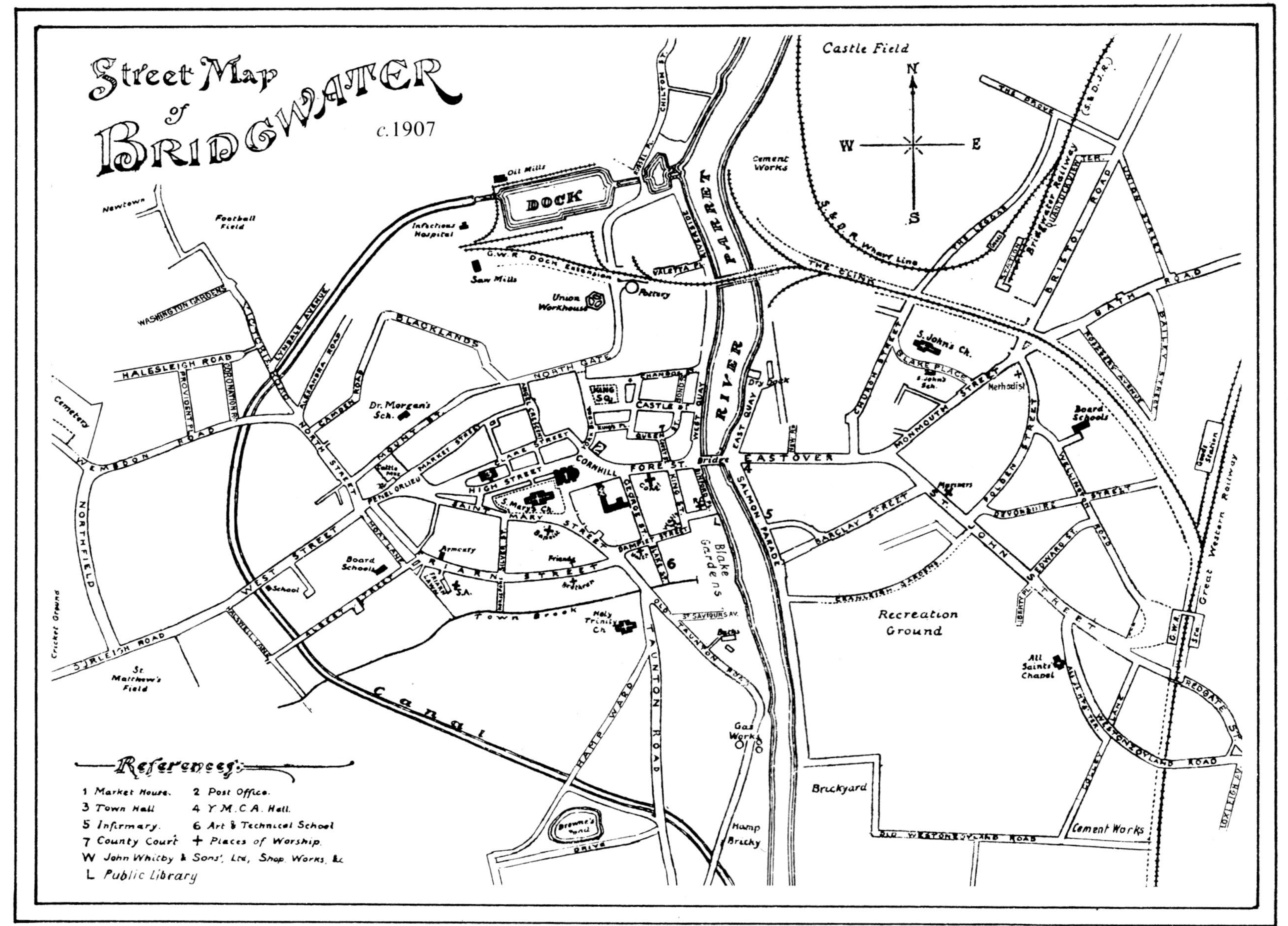
Street Map of Bridgwater
c.1907
References:
1 Market House. 2 Post Office.
3 Town Hall 4 Y.M.C.A. Hall.
5 Infirmary. 6 Art & Technical School
7 County Court + Places of Worship.
W John Whitby & Sons' Ltd, Shop Works, &c.
L Public Library
Castle Field
N
W
E
S
Cement Works
Dock
Oil Mills
Infectious Hospital
Saw Mills
Union Workhouse
Pottery
River Parrett
Recreation Ground
Blake Gardens
Canal
Brickyard
Cement Works
Great Western Railway
Goods Station
S. John's Ch.
Board Schools
All Saints' Chapel
Holy Trinity Ch.
Dr. Morgan's Sch.
Football Field
Newtown
Cemetery
Cricket Ground
St. Matthew's Field
Gas Works
Hamp Brickyard
Browne's Pond
Eastover
Salmon Parade
Taunton Road
North Street
West Street
High Street
Cornhill
Fore St.
Bristol Road
Bath Road
Monmouth Street
Northfield
Wembdon Road
Blacklands
North Gate

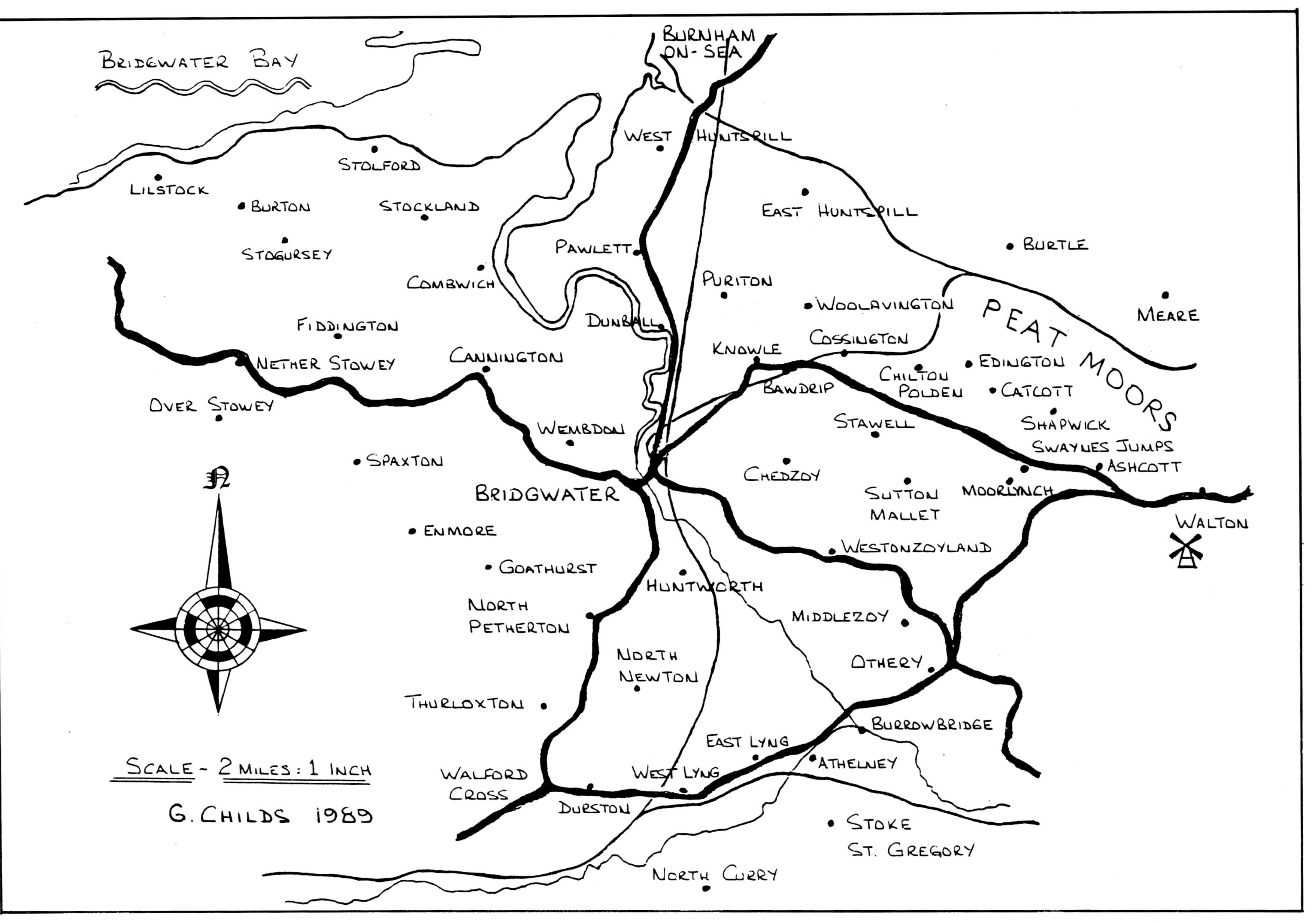

Bridgewater Bay
Burnham On-Sea
West Huntspill
Stolford
Lilstock
Burton
Stockland
Stogursey
East Huntspill
Burtle
Pawlett
Combwich
Puriton
Woolavington
Meare
Dunball
Peat Moors
Fiddington
Cossington
Knowle
Edington
Nether Stowey
Cannington
Chilton Polden
Catcott
Bawdrip
Over Stowey
Stawell
Shapwick
Wembdon
Swaynes Jumps
Ashcott
Spaxton
Chedzoy
Bridgwater
Sutton Mallet
Moorlynch
Walton
Enmore
Westonzoyland
Goathurst
Huntworth
North Petherton
Middlezoy
North Newton
Othery
Thurloxton
Burrowbridge
East Lyng
Athelney
Scale - 2 Miles : 1 Inch
Walford Cross
West Lyng
G. Childs 1989
Durston
Stoke St. Gregory
North Curry

FOREWORD

Bygone Bridgwater and the Villages gave enormous pleasure to all who are interested in the history of Bridgwater and its surrounding area. So much has changed over the years and yet with the help of the excellent photographs one could see again on all sides reminders of those earlier years.

I am, therefore, all the more delighted that Rod Fitzhugh and Will Loudon have returned to the task with this further edition of *More Bygone Bridgwater and the Villages.* I know it will give great pleasure to very many people and I congratulate them once again on their imagination and hard work, which contributed to making the first edition such a success and which I am sure will be reflected again in this new publication.

THE RT. HON. TOM KING, M.P.
House of Commons
4 April 1989

INTRODUCTION

In today's world the postcard is a novelty, usually sent to relatives and friends from a holiday venue, but from the time the postcard came into being when launched on the world on 1st October 1869 from a Post Office in Vienna, it has had very many other uses. When few had telephones and post was collected and delivered within hours rather than days, it was the postcard that served as the quickest means of communication, many cards at the turn of the century carrying messages such as "I will be round for tea this afternoon". Other cards were used for greetings for Christmas, and other seasonal or family events, whilst shopkeepers and traders found them a useful advertising medium. It was in 1872 that this country authorised its first postcard postal service, but only the address was permitted on the 'blank' side, and senders found space around the picture for any message. Those cards were smaller than the ones we know today, and were called 'Court cards', the larger size coming into being on 1st November 1899, when the famous publishers Raphael Tuck and Sons launched their first cards. Not until 1902 were messages allowed alongside on a 'divided back' design, but such was the need for a cheap and easy means of communication that at the start of the First World War there were an average of 2 million postcards sent daily. Those interested in deltiology, the hobby of collecting postcards, say that after 1918 the use of the postcard declined, probably as the direct result of the cost of a stamp increasing to one penny! Therefore it is between 1895 and say 1930 that one finds so many photographic postcards of such interest to the historian of any locality, depicting the dramatic changes in fashion, way of life and social system at a pace not previously known in history. From the large hats, buttoned boots, pinched waists and long skirts for women, aprons and sailor suits for the children, altering only slightly in years after the turn of the century, one moves to the small hats and shortening skirts from 1914 onwards. A great divide existed between the rich and poor, town and county, nobility and upper classes and those below; only the workhouse and charity were available for the desperate, destitute and disadvantaged, and the mixing and intermarrying between groups was a scandal. Families were large, but experienced a slower pace of life with few distractions and man-made amusements; communities remained close-knit and neighbours helped each other at times of death and disaster, many an orphaned child of urban life being 'taken in' and brought up by those who lived next door or opposite, there being no Social Services Department to take such youngsters into the care of the Local Authority. The hurtling pace of industry and then the Great War changed lives and attitudes, and another war 1939-45 yet again altered the landscape of shire and spire and the lives of villagers and townsfolk alike. The postcard photographers, first on glass plates and then on film, captured those at work and leisure, grand and simple events, occasions of happiness and sadness. Much may have changed since then, but there are those still alive who can remember people, places, processions and so on, a veritable making of history in their lifetime! By demolition and development many places and areas have become unrecognisable. Whether the present is preferable to the past is a matter for debate elsewhere, but is essential that cameos of social history in one form or another are preserved, to be considered and compared with the past, both now and by future generations. Many family photographs gathering dust in attics, when removed from the album and turned over, may well be postcards, for that was the vogue. If you recognise the people or the place, the date or the event, then do make a pencil note on the back, or contact me or Will Loudon, since I am sure that we would be very interested, and will be happy to help you in any way. The increasing number of postcards in our respective collections prompted me with the help of Will Loudon to publish *Bygone Bridgwater and the Villages,* which we launched somewhat nervously in October 1987. It was produced for our own personal satisfaction and to ensure the pictures of the area could be shared rather than secreted away in a cupboard. We were not sure that anyone else would be interested and its success has been both a surprise and pleasure to us both. Avidly we have followed its rise and fall in the local bestsellers book chart in the *Bridgwater Mercury and Somerset Express* as supplied by Keith Hardy of Rhyme and Reason in High Street. The demand since 1987 has been a source of delight and a tribute to our wives without whose help, patience and understanding it would have never seen the light of day. Our interest kindled, and then fuelled with material unpublished or subsequently collected, we decided to venture forth again with *More Bygone Bridgwater and the Villages.* To all those who showed such interest before, in the hope that they will find similar interest in the following pages, we express our grateful thanks. In particular we would thank the many people who have written to us with information, enquiries and comments about our first effort as authors, since it is as the result of such interest and moral support that this second book is now a reality. Finally our very sincere thanks to the Right Honourable Tom King, M.P., whose complimentary letter after reading the first edition is a proud possession, and whose offer to write the foreword to this book is deeply appreciated.

ROD FITZHUGH

DEDICATED TO
those early photographers of the Bridgwater area who, through the lens of a camera, captured sights and scenes, creating a pictorial record as a lasting image of the past.

THE TOWN

THE AUTHENTIC
ARMS OF BRIDGWATER.

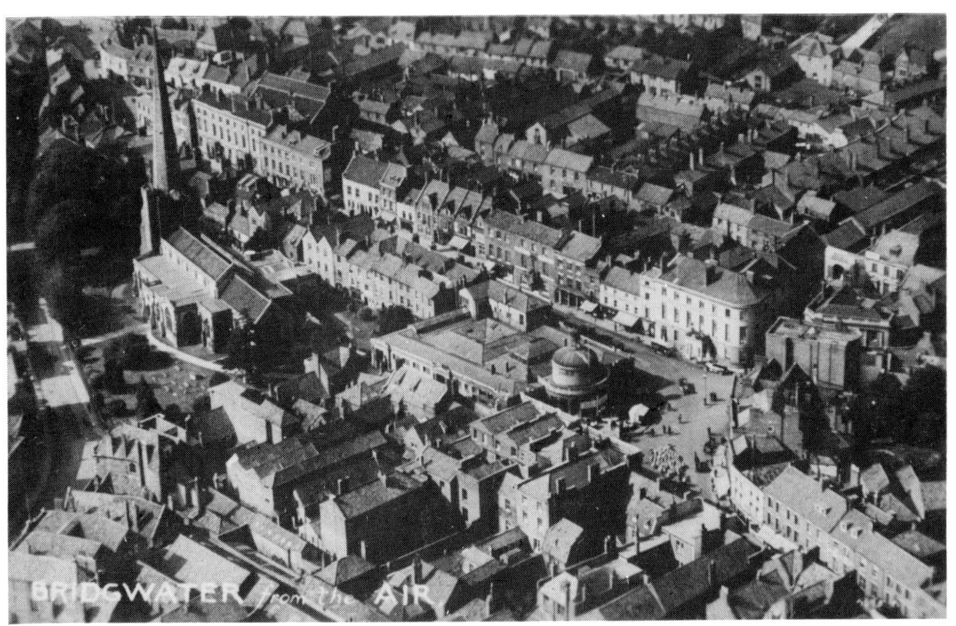

c. 1933 Aerial view of the town
During the late 1920's and early 1930's with the development of more sophisticated aircraft and cameras, aerial photographic views of towns became popular. Bridgwater was no exception and a selection of half a dozen scenes was issued at around this time. In this view, the camerman focused his lens on the Cornhill, St. Mary's Church and High Street – how the north side of High Street has changed since then!.

7441 HIGH STREET, BRIDGWATER

c. 1906 High Sreet
Published by Kingsway, this card shows an everyday scene at the start of the century with visitors arriving by horse-drawn carriage at the Royal Clarence Hotel as it was then known, the most important hostelry in the area, and the social meeting point of the gentry and wealthy.

The Clarence Hotel, Bridgwater

c. 1920 High Street
Another view of the Royal Clarence Hotel, this time by an unknown publisher, but showing Taylor's Restaurant and also the premises of Brooks' Dye Works Ltd. further up the street at number 6. It is perhaps the transport halted outside the hotel that remains of puzzling interest, for example, to whom did the lovely landaulet belong, and just what was likely to be in those sacks on the delivery waggon with the unattended horse?

High St, Bridgwater. 2876-31

c. 1930 High Street
The Bull & Butcher public house at number 26 was next door to William Smith, saddler and harness manufacturer, at number 24 with the old established firm of B.E. Radford, outfitter, at number 22 and 'Ye Old Oak Inne' beyond. It is just possible to see the sign of Elliott & Son family butchers at number 20. The modern development of the Angel shopping precinct makes this old view nothing more than a memory, and an example of local history.

c. 1905 High Street
Gas came to Bridgwater some thirty years before the Town Hall was opened in 1865, but well illuminated the building designed by local surveyor, Mr. C. Knowles. This was an imposing edifice housing municipal meeting-rooms, council offices, the town library and criminal courts, the latter being both borough and Quarter Sessions. The Town Hall incorporated a main galleried hall capable of seating 1200 people, and was in all a building of which Bridgwater was justly proud.

c. 1905 Fore Street from Cornhill
The statue of Admiral Blake on the Cornhill, his right hand pointing in the direction in which some eighty years later he has been re-sited. The Home and Colonial Stores at 21 Cornhill and the premises of E.W. Hill, linen draper at number 11 are only memories today.

c. 1911 Fore Street
Looking towards the town bridge, with the Wilts. and Dorset Bank on the right and the adjacent premises at 15 Cornhill of Best & Co. clothiers. On the next corner (interestingly now 'Next') was the well known store of Walter Belcher, stationer and bookseller, postcard printer and publisher. china and glass dealer, W.J. Curry had premises at number 16 and the boot and shoe maker George Oliver was at numbers 17 and 18.

c. 1905 Eastover
Looking down Eastover, standing on the town bridge and with Salmon Parade and East Quay to the right and left, at the time when Vowles and Co., provision merchants at York House were selling tea at 1s. 4d. a lb. A small boy attired in stiff collar stands, apparently examining his change, a dog patiently stops and stares, and no one appears in any danger from the traffic, it being the people on the pavement or in the street who make the scene a busy one.

F. CULLIFORD
Late E. CULLIFORD,
28 High Street & Clare Street
BRIDGWATER.

Cabinet Maker, Carver, Upholsterer, & General Undertaker

Dealer in all kinds of Antique Furniture.

Repairs and Restoration of every description of Furniture undertaken.

All kinds of Carved Oak Church Work undertaken, Pulpits, Screens, Etc.

EST 1862

W. H. SMITH,
High St., Bridgwater

SADDLER AND BAG MANUFACTURER.
ALL KINDS OF TRAVELLING BAGS.
REPAIRS A SPECIALITY.

c. 1905 Eastover
The man needed by the wealthy and the poor, Mr. P.G. Edwards, jeweller but also pawnbroker, had a well used shop at 6 Eastover. Opposite at number 11 and outside the premises of Messrs. I. & V. Parsons, ironmongers rope makers and ship chandlers, is an interesting handcart. Examining the scene closely, one can see two policeman, perhaps quietly patrolling Eastover and keeping a watchful eye on the people about as they approach the showrooms of the Bridgwater Furnishing Company on the corner of New Road.

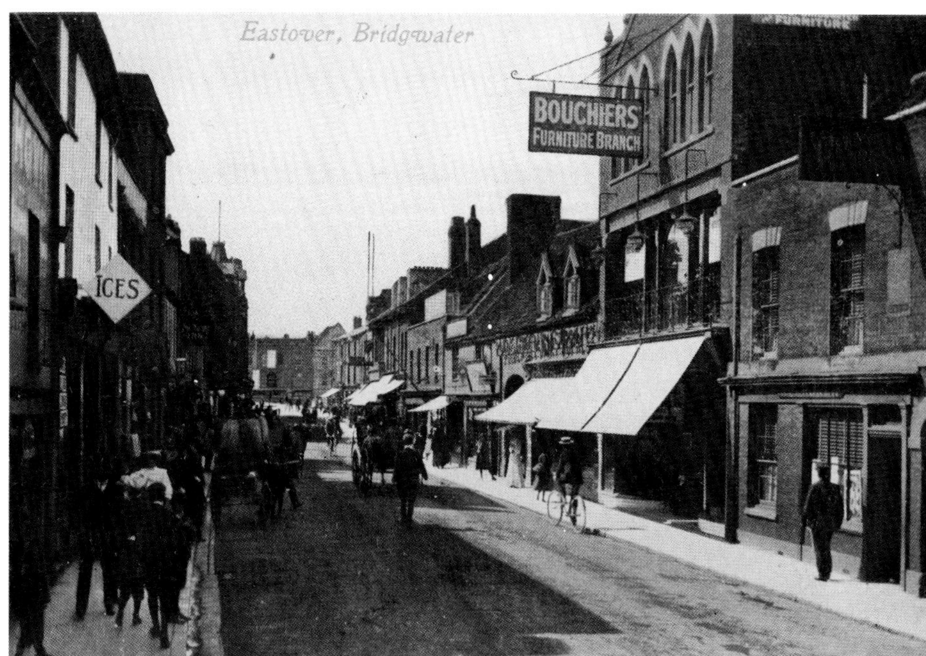

c. 1909 Eastover
At number 41 the sign over the shop reads 'Polden Hill Dairy Farm Produce Depot' where Edward Butcher was the manager at the time of this photograpic postcard. Next door at number 43 was Bouchiers, the well known local house furnishers, adjacent to the Devonshire Arms public house, which closed its doors in 1963.

c. 1903 Eastover
An early postcard of a quiet and almost deserted Eastover looking east, taken when signwriters were preparing an imposing fascia for Vowles & Co., at York House on the corner of East Quay. On the right were the premises of watchmaker, Mr.J. Sanders whose window appears to be occluded with sunblinds.

c. 1920 Town Bridge
A crowd of thirsty men outside the Punch Bowl Inn eagerly awaits opening time. The picture can be dated from the appeal sign referred to below which is just visible under the dome of the Cornhill. The Punch Bowl on West Quay closed in 1964, but Barclays Bank on the corner of Binford Place had an even briefer residence, showing rarely on postcards. John Hamlin & Son were well known grocers with their premises at 4/6 Fore Street.

c. 1903 Town Bridge
Twenty years after it was built the bridge was already the traditional gathering place for local men on a sunny day. The YMCA building constructed in 1887 stood on the corner of Salmon Parade but sadly had a lifespan of only 81 years before it was demolished in 1968.

c. 1920 Cornhill

A postcard of interest both to Bridgwater and to enthusiasts of motor transport because of the solid tyred, open topped motor bus with its exterior staircase to the upper deck, shown here at the bus terminus in the Cornhill and picking up passengers for Taunton and stops en route. The appeal board attached to the pillars of the Cornhill dome attracted public subscriptions to finance the memorial to the fallen from Bridgwater in the First World War subsequently erected in King Square and dedicated on 25th September 1924.

c. 1928 Fore Street

A busy scene with horses, carts, bicycles and lots of people, but of even greater interest is the early Pratts Spirit lorry with its front-opening windscreen, parked outside the premises of David Greig, Provision Merchant at number 40 in the foreground of his card. Adjacent, but just into the Cornhill, were the shoemakers Olivers with the distinctive shop sign overhanging the street. Davis & Son, house furnishers at 27 Fore Street and 5 George Sreet had protruding from their premises the suspended lantern, then a familiar form of street lighting.

c. 1909 Cornhill

An animated scene shown on a fine example of a photographic postcard and a favourite of the collection. The delivery van belonged jointly to the South Western & Midland Railway Companies and the Somerset & Dorset Joint Railway. Horses amble, young lads linger, an obvious moment when time was not of the essence! It was in 1826 that the Market Hall buildings and the landmark dome on the Cornhill were built by a Mr. Thomas Hutchings of Bridgwater, well known for the other buildings of note for which he was responsible, including College House in North Street where he lived, the National Provincial Bank and Hutchings Buildings in Mount Street.

c. 1903 Taunton Road
An early postcard published by George Comer of 35 Eastover and first printed in black and white but subsequently with a hand-tinted blue sky. The cameraman stood on the canal bridge looking towards the town, with neither man nor beast, let alone traffic, anywhere in sight.

c. 1910 St.Mary's Street
Marycourt with its beautiful carved oak and stone frontage, the reputed residence of Judge Jeffries and a street little changed in eighty years.

c. 1910 Fore Street
A particularly clear view of the detailed interior of the Congregational Church, built in 1862 and demolished after 100 years when a new Church was built in West Street. The interior of the Fore Street Church was highly decorative with its spiral pillars and ornamental galleries. Around the arch surrounding the organ pipes were painted the words "Draw nigh to God and He will draw nigh to you". From God to mammon, the site was redeveloped with a supermarket!

c. 1910 Penel Orlieu
The coat of arms of the Tynte family appears within the sign of the Tynte Arms public house to the immediate left of this view, a hostelry known later as the Blue Boar. Bridges and Son, printers and stationers, had premises at number 34, with Mr.W. Crocker, tailor and outfitter next door. The writer of this postcard says that she was at the time staying at the house with an "X", and then apologised for smudging the "X"!

c. 1910 Friarn Street
A rare postcard view of the entrance to Friarn Street from St. Mary Sreet with everyone standing still for the benefit of the photographer. The large hoardings on the wall of the Rose & Crown advertise the Coventry-manufactured Humber and Rudge Whitworth cycles obtainable from the garage of Real Medland & Wills. Veritas gas mantles and the Somerset & Dorset railway excursions to Bath and Bournemouth share the billing.

c. 1905 Cornhill
The Blake statue provided a focal point for the handcart vendors of ice cream and wafers. The photographer on this occasion has well captured the atmosphere of a hot summer's day on the paved area in front of the Corn Exchange when a water ice would have been most welcome.

48 ADVERTISEMENTS—BRIDGWATER.

Telegrams—Thompson Bros., Bridgwater.

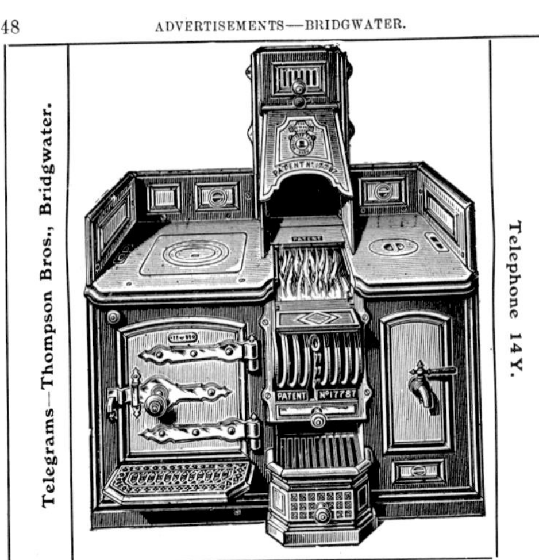

Telephone 14Y.

THOMPSON BROS.,
CORNHILL, BRIDGWATER.

Furnishing & General Ironmongers.

GRATES, RANGES, MANTELS, HEARTHS, KERBS, to suit all purchasers.

Hot and Cold Water, Gas, and Electrical Engineers.
TELEPHONE WORK, &c., estimated for.

10 per cent. (2/- in the £) off all marked prices for cash.

BOOK AND STATIONERY DEPT.

JOHN WHITBY & SONS, Ltd., Est. 1834.

BOOKSELLERS, NEWSAGENTS,
STATIONERS (Wholesale & Retail),
PRINTERS, ILLUMINATORS, &c.
Artists' Materials. Goss China. Fancy Goods.
MUSIC & MUSICAL INSTRUMENT DEALERS.

MUSIC DEPT.

c. 1906 the Town Library
A drawing of the proposed library published in postcard form some months before the official opening of the building itself on 20th September 1906, giving local people an idea in advance of the design and perhaps also indicating the importance of the library to the community. The library was constructed to the plans of local architect E. Godfrey Page (son of E.T. Page, photographer and local publisher) on the site of Binford House, the previous residence of Mr.R.C. Else, a former Mayor of the town. It cost £3500 to construct, the money being donated by the world famous Carnegie Foundation. The library was officially opened by the Mayor, Mr.H.W. Pollard, after a civic procession from the Council Chamber. It was a grand occasion with many speeches, after which guests were invited to take refreshments in a large marquee erected in nearby Blake Gardens.

c. 1906
The entrance hall of the Bridgwater Public Library soon after the official opening, this postcard being the work of William Belcher of Fore Street. More recently the library has been extended, refurbished and computerised!

c. 1912 Durleigh Road
The placid leafy look of Durleigh Road, a postcard view published by Judges of Hastings. Clearly visible in the distance is the spire of St. Mary's Church with the Horse and Jockey public house on the right. This was a postcard view that remained a favourite for years as evidenced by the postmark of 1938.

c. 1907 Rosebery Avenue
Just off Bath Road with houses typical of those constructed to the demand created by the opportunities for employment in Bridgwater at the turn of the century. A situation facing the railway lines and goods trains running from the docks and river wharf to link up with the main line at the GWR station proved no distraction to occupiers of the properties. Although built to meet an immediate need, building design of the day still demanded ornamental lintels and window surrounds and standards that stood the test of time to the present day.

c. 1908 Lyndale Avenue.
A view taken by Montague Cooper, with a secondary interest, namely the message on the reverse. The writer was none other than the lady alongside the lamp post with an unusual turn of phrase, and her tale bears relating in her own words and style: "Dear Miss Reed, this is the Avenue we live in. I am just by our gate I'm errand boy for the time being going up with some buns and as all the male Bakers were out of town as it was their Annual outing for that day why I was obliged to take them so that they should not be disappointed, we were holding a sale of work in aid of our Church funds up at Haygrove Hill House grounds on the Durleigh Road we had promised the buns for the refreshments before we knew the men were going away its the men, not the masters they don't go but all of the group have gone to Stowey". A female errand "boy" one could not refer to today!

c. 1915 Salmon Parade
This scene of the imposing entrance to Bridgwater Infirmary features the little white dog which belonged to the Matron, Miss Evelyne Kitching. A new front elevation and the portico had been erected in 1876, together with a new ward 'The Poole Ward' in memory of Gabriel Stone Poole who had died that year, the cost being met by public subscription.

c. 1906 Bristol and Bath Roads
A steam roller with its road gang make an impressive sight on the junction of Bristol Road and Bath Road. The water-filled trough in the foreground was a vital necessity both for horse-drawn vehicles and steam engines. It was on the triangle of land behind the steam roller that the famous cannon stood until the late 1930's. The 'x' above houses in Bath Road indicates the sender's home.

c. 1910 Northfield

Walter Belcher of Fore Street produced and published a number of photographic town centre street scenes, including this one of Northfield, although on this postcard marked Northfields. Whilst relatively unexciting as a photograph postcards like this are a rare find today, and to the collector and town enthusiast alike, a valuable pictorial record of the area at the time.

c. 1903 Blake Place

St. John's Church viewed from Blake Place with the original iron railings surrounding the churchyard. How this area has changed in recent years with all the new buildings and roads in place of the demolished vicarage, school and church hall – all in the cause of progress, although there are those who would disagree.

c. 1905 Blake Gardens

The pillared entrance to Blake Gardens from Dampiet Street, little changed over eighty years later. The writer of the card advises the recipient "going to Puriton Sunday School Union Meeting tomorrow."

c. 1912 Mansion House Lane
To obtain this view of the White Lion Hotel at 29 High Street, the photographer would have set up his camera equipment in front of the fire station opened six years earlier, and sadly now no more. The tower of St. Mary's Church, an additional feature of the photograph, was built of red sandstone from Wembdon, the construction starting on 28th June 1368 using scaffolding wood from the Royal foresst of Petherton. To create the contrast, fawn coloured Ham Hill stone was used for the spire, a landmark for miles around.

c. 1905 Angel Crescent
This superb photographic postcard by an unknown photographer perhaps is the pride of the collection of street scenes, the quality of reproduction adding further to its value. The delivery cart, so typical of the day, is parked close to the archway which formed the rear entrance to the courtyard of the Bristol Hotel in High Street. The beautiful facade of Angel Crescent has been preserved for posterity within the new Angel Place development, where imaginatively the past faces the future.

c. 1905 Hamp Pond
The peaceful scene of Hamp Pond, just off the west side of the Taunton Road approaching Bridgwater, sometimes called Browne's Pond. The former brickyard of John Browne was nearby.

c. 1908 Blake Gardens
The leafy shade on a hot summer's day proved a welcome attraction to a lot of people.

c. 1906 Blake Gardens
A view rarely taken by photographers of the time, who apparently preferred to take pictures of the gardens showing the other side of the arch window, which was erected there after being discarded by a church some time earlier. The window arch was demolished in the late 1960's, but the bandstand erected in 1908 remains a familiar sight to this day.

c. 1904 Blake Street
Then known as Blake House, the birthplace of Admiral Robert Blake in 1598, thc property became a home for the Blake museum in 1924 and houses a fine collection of personal possessions and memorabilia of Bridgwater's famous son, together with documents and artefacts relating to the battle of Sedgemoor, as well as historical town records.

c. 1910 Taunton Road
A view of Holy Trinity Church built in 1839, taken from Taunton Road looking towards St. Mary's Church with its famous spire just visible in the distance. Holy Trinity, with its interesting external bell tower, was demolished in 1958 when Broadway was constructed.

c. 1906 St. Mary Street
The typical advertising signs of the time, this time outside the cycle and motor garage premises of Real Medland and Wills on the corner of Dampiet Street, but with no cycles or motors in sight!

c. 1912
The United Methodist Church on the corner of Monmouth Street and Eastover, a building which has changed little in outward appearance over the years. The site was acquired for £1,338 and on it the Church was constructed at a cost of £3000. It was officially opened by Mrs R.A. Sanders, wife of the town's Conservative Member of Parliament, and Mr.Joseph Butler of Bristol. Sadly the beautiful gas lamp in the middle of the road has not been preserved and the wall and iron railings were not replaced when Monmouth Street at this junction was widened many years ago.

c. 1914 Wembdon Church
This peaceful study of the church and school as the storm clouds of approaching war gathered over Europe was the work of Montague Cooper who had electric and daylight studios producing instantaneous photographs in Bridgwater, Taunton, Burnham and Lynton.

c. 1908 Wembdon
The post office at the bottom of Wembdon Hill, long before the road was hard surfaced with tarmacadam when riding a bicycle was a precarious occupation! Not that long ago a new post office was built adjoining the house, enabling the shop shown here to be incorporated within the living rooms, a bay window replacing the doorway.

c. 1913 Wembdon Road
At a time when motor vehicles were a preserve of the wealthy, photographer J. Phillips of 99 John Street experienced no danger or problems in setting up his camera equipment in the middle of Wembdon Road to capture a scene devoid of movement, an impossible daylight task seventy six years later. To the left is what was originally.one of the four toll houses, the others being in Taunton Road, Monmouth Sreet and Durleigh Road.

c. 1910 Wembdon Hill
Trees today obscure this view of the houses on Wembdon Hill, photographed by Wood & Son of 20 Cornhill in 1910.

c. 1906 Wembdon Fields
What secrets were exchanged by these two young ladies as they paused on the footbridge over the stream in the seclusion of the surrounding willows.....?

EARNING A LIVING

c. 1927 St. John Street
Supplied by the local brewery, Starkey Knight & Ford, at a time when William Bradbury was the licensee, the Crown Inn at 96 St. John Street shown in this photographic postcard was deriving additional income from the Bridgwater Empire in allowing it to advertise its programme features, this particular week being "Flaming Waters". Interestingly the shop opposite was advertising for sale a solid oak bedroom suite by Jays of Bristol for the princely sum of ten guineas, then a month's wages at least for the working man, and perhaps proportionately not that far removed from today's equivalent.

A. H. GALLEY,

7, Bath Road
and
Monmouth
Street,
Bridgwater.

MANUFACTURER OF ALL KINDS OF
Plain & Fancy CARDBOARD BOXES.
Draper's Stock and Fixture Boxes to Order.

c. 1913 Cornhill
The imposing facade of Fox Fowler & Co., bankers at 24/25 Cornhill established as far back as 1787, with the offices of Louis Lovibond Solicitor, and J. & A.W.Sully & Co., Chartered Accountants, all names that can be read in the windows over the arches. A building of proportion and significance, but like so many in the town demolished for so called 'better things'.

c. 1906 West Quay

A card which, although printed rather than photographic, is a superb addition to the collection, this time showing clearly Ekers store at 4/5 West Quay, its windows reflecting the shipping moored in the river alongside the roadway. The store displayed advertisements typical of the time for the sale of prams, mail carts, bedsteads, Bradbury's sewing machines, furnishing and upholstery – as well as providing an undertakers and funeral service. The words beneath the card are worthy of repetition as an example of media 'hype' of the day, "Our Furniture Is record Value, a trial Order is Respectfully Solicited by H. Ekers, Complete Furnisher, West Quay, Bridgwater."

Our Furniture Isrecord Value, a Trial Order is Respectfully Solicited by H. Ekers, Complete Furnisher, West Quay, Bridgwater

c. 1907

9 Penel Orlieu and the truly magnificent display of meat and poultry by butcher William Pitman, a sight rarely, if ever, seen today, but captured as a record of the past by local photographer J. Vearncombe who had a studio nearby at 29 Penel Orlieu.

c. 1920
A view of the interior of Hamlins Tudor Café at 21 St. Mary Street, typical tea rooms frequented and enjoyed by the genteel. How easy it is to imagine the cucumber sandwiches and home-made cakes, as well as the news and gossip of the day!

c. 1906
A superb recent addition to the collection, showing both the magnificent frontage of 'Crokers', the tea and coffee rooms of Henry Croker at 44 Eastover, and the typical children's clothing of the time as youngsters pose in the doorway – with the additional face at the window of a little boy perhaps too young to be included in the scene below, since it may well have been that Mr. J.C. Hosier "Photo Artist of Bridgwater" was commissioned to take this study to record the special display of Cadbury's Chocolate. Mr. Croker was well known in Eastover for his bread and confectionery, probably never thinking that a photographic postcard of his shop would be so interesting to a collector over eighty years later.

Price 10/6, 15/-, 21/- and upwards.

Fresh Cut Flowers and Floral Designs

OF EVERY DESCRIPTION TO ORDER AT SHORTEST NOTICE.

HAYWARD BROS., *Seedsmen, Florists aad Fruiterers,*

Cornhill & Trinity Cottage, Taunton Road, BRIDGWATER.

c. 1905
December 16th 1905 is the postmark of this advertising card of Hayward Bros., Seedsmen, Florists and Fruiterers, quoting addresses of Trinity Cottage, Taunton Road, and Cornhill, although the latter in fact was 5 High Street. The reverse message requested Miss Tratt of Catcott to supply variegated holly, undoubtedly for the festive season. At the prices shown, in 1905, it is obvious that "Fresh cut flowers and Floral Designs – of every description to order at shortest notice" were a luxury for the wealthy, if one equates them with inflation from then to now.

c. 1911
Frequently postcards were produced as an advertising medium and here local photographers Squibbs & Carey were commissioned to produce the publicity material for the White Hart Hotel at 48 Eastover, making known Good Accommodation for Motorists, Next to Garage, terms Moderate, and with Wines, Spirits & Cigars of the Best Quality, and the proprietor Mr.R.A. Bacon so confident of those words, that he added his name. Can anyone add to the writing on front and back "This is very good think not" and "Lest we Forget Bank Holiday Aug. 1907 4p.m."? One is left with many unanswered questions....!

c. 1904
11 Fore Street and second from the right proudly stands George White the butcher, but this card has an added interest, having been sent by his wife to a Mr.A. Nuttycombe at Jones Farm, Chilton Polden, with a message relating to the provision of meat in which she says "My Husband left B'water this Morning & will not be back for a few days, so I cannot send for the sheep today it was four o'clock when your letter came if you are in town tomorrow you can bring them in or leave them until my husband comes home".

c.1905
The tiled front of Frank Holley, East End Meat Supply at 28 Eastover, a card used by him on this occasion to order a supply of rib of beef from Mr.E. Gooding of Penzoy Farm, Westonzoyland.

c. 1910
The scene of a carpenters' workshop where five craftsmen and an apprentice proudly display their hand-made furniture in the days before mass production. Sadly no details are recorded on this postcard taken by Bridgwater photographer H.L. Slocombe to enable identification of the men or the location, but hopefully a reader may recognise someone and come forward to solve the mystery.

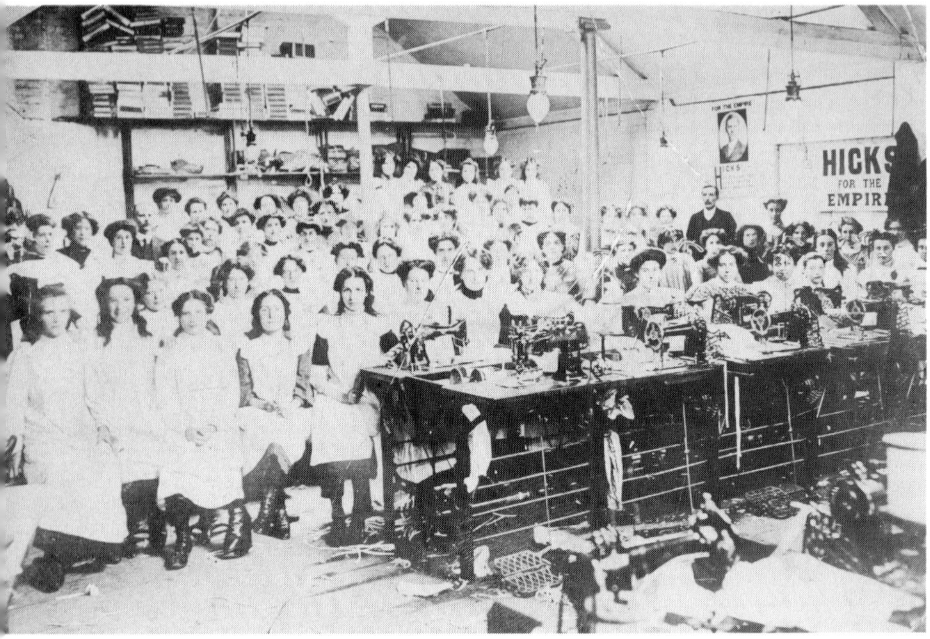

c. 1910
The election poster for Liberal candidate Mr. H. Hicks appears to date this postcard to 1910, since on 20th January he was not elected as Member of Parliament for Bridgwater, losing to his Conservative opponent, Mr. R.A. Sanders, by 1679 votes, but then on 7th December of the same year and in another general election the same result occurred, Mr Hicks losing this time by 1381 votes. Given the sewing machines, the fabric on the shelves to the rear, perhaps this photographic postcard by Mr. H.L. Slocombe was taken inside one of the shirt factories in Bridgwater at the time, but which, and whose factory?

c. 1908
Eight solemn young men pictured at work in Bridgwater's then labour intensive brick and tile industry and when it was the major source of employment in the area. The identity of the men, dog and brickyard, remains a mystery, but it is the wheelbarrow that identifies the occupation, since the style of barrow on which the men in front are seated was typical of those designed for and used during all the brick and tile processes, from the digging of clay, drying to kiln firing.

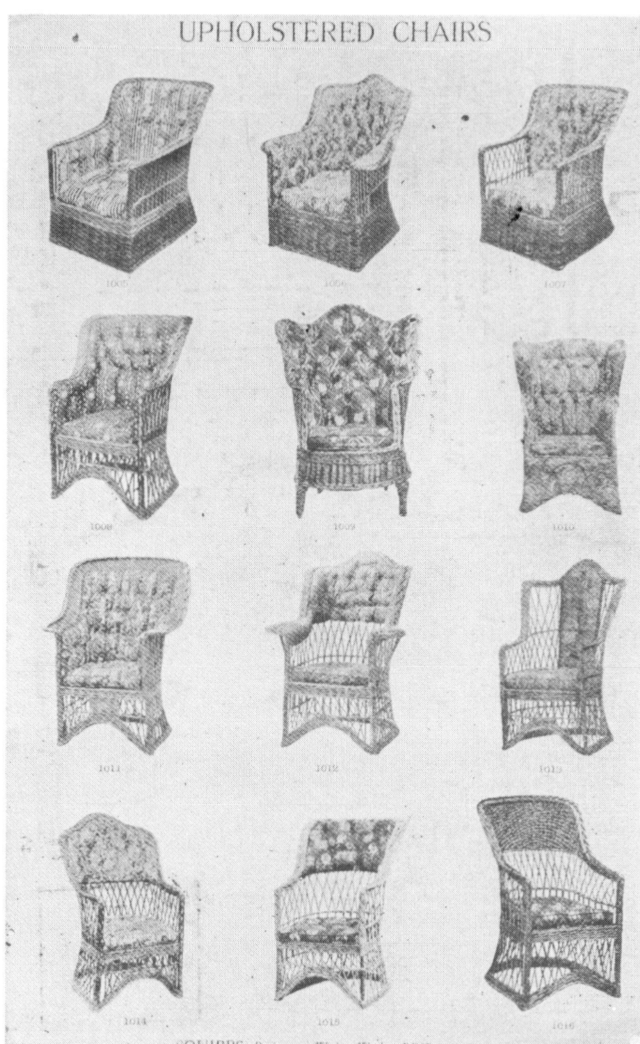

c. 1912
The Bridgwater Wicker Works Ltd. produced furniture at 16 Mount Street and this postcard, from the message on the other side, suggests that a sale was to take place, using the interesting phrase "job clearance sale reductions". Perhaps in some ways times have not changed! The upholstered cane chair shown in the top left hand corner was sold in 3 sizes, 20 inch at 49s. each, 24 inch at 59s. each or 30 inch at 75s. each. The cheapest chair, the 18 inch shown in the bottom right hand corner, was 19s.

COALS ! !

GEORGE BRYANT
& SON.

Coal, Coke, Corn, Cake, Salt, and Manure Merchants.

IF NOT SATISFIED WITH YOUR COAL MERCHANT WHY NOT TRY US?

Best attention to all enquiries.

Offices:
6 and 8, Clare Street,
BRIDGWATER.

c.1908
Have you tried Mustad Bright Pointed Horse Nails They are the Best – urges this splendid advertising card, noting the local agent, Thompson Bros. Ironmongers. Whatever the merits of Mustad, it is beyond dispute that Thompsons have served Bridgwater for almost two hundred years, having been established in 1797 and remaining ironmongers for the town serving its needs in that and in other allied ways from then to now, a record hard to beat.

15th October 1908
Local devotees of golf will recognise this postcard as a small but significant reminder of the day the sport came to Bridgwater. For years enthusiasts travelled to Berrow and to Cannington, but following proposals of well known local dental surgeon Mr. W. Herbert Phillips, every effort was made to obtain links for the town, eventually purchased at Haygrove on the Durleigh Road where a 'commodious' pavilion was erected. Over one hundred people immediately became members of the club, and on the important date of 15th October 1908 Mr. H.H.P. Bouverie made the first drive, using a club borrowed from Mr. J.H. Taylor, the well known mid-Surrey golf professional, and by repute a household name in the golf world of 1908. This particular photographic shows the inside of the refreshment tent where Mr. R. Bagg, who had 'dining room' premises at 20 Fore Street, provided all that was necessary for the inner man of players, guests and members of the committee.

c. 1907
The steam traction engine of William John Bunter, a hauling contractor of 13/15 Dampiet Street, photographed alongside a building site and with some of the workmen having come down from the wooden scaffolding to pose in front of this metal wheeled engine and trailer. Apart from the noise of house building, the combination of engine and trailer must have been quite deafening.

SPECIAL OCCASIONS

1918 General Election
A crowd of people assembled outside the offices of the *Bridgwater Mercury,* then in High Street, just after the results of the December 1918 General Election had been announced. Conservative Lt. Colonel R.A. Sanders was elected, polling 12,587 votes as against 5,771 of his Labour opponent, Mr. S.J. Plummer. This postcard is interesting for another reason, since it is obvious that when the photograph was processed the figures on the notice posted on the *Mercury* offices did not show up clearly, and the photographer chose to enhance the negative by writing the figures in himself. However, in so doing he made a mistake in his subtraction, for the majority should have been 6,816 and not as he showed it!

1906 General Election
26th January and crowds gathered outside the Town Hall for the declaration of the poll when Liberal candidate, Mr. H.G. Montgomery, was elected to Parliament with the slim majority of seventeen votes over his Conservative opponent,. Mr. R.A. Sanders.

1906/7 Bridgwater Albion Football Club
A picture that tells all – the date, the event, the team and the name of each individual – would that all cards were so informative.

1910/11
Montague Cooper captured this critical point in the water polo match between Bridgwater and Yeovil just as Radmilovic scored. A new grandstand for the pool had not long been completed for the protection of the spectators, both from rain and splash!

1908
The Taunton Road football ground and the ten players, goalkeeper and linesmen pose for the customary group photograph of the Bridgwater and Albion Association Football team.

1909
The annual July street procession in aid of Bridgwater Hospital Saturday Fund, seen here crossing the town bridge. Resplendent in gleaming livery, the carriages and well groomed horses pull their VIP occupants, whilst local fire officers on foot add further colour and local participation. This charity event always attracted large crowds willing to give their pennies for such a worthy cause in the days well before the National Health Service.

22nd June 1911
The Bridgwater Coronation procession entering High Street from Cornhill and another postcard clearly showing female fashion of the time.

15th July 1936
The band of the Argyll and Sutherland Highlanders with "pipers an' all" conducted by Mr. A.C. O'Connor marching from Cornhill into High Street. By permission of Lt. Colonel H.J.D. Clark M.C., the pipers headed a procession of those invited to the opening ceremonies of the Odeon Cinema in Penel Orlieu, performed by Mr. R.P.Croom-Johnson K.C., Member of Parliament for Bridgwater. Described as a 'super cinema', the Odeon was designed by a Nottingham architect, Mr.T. Cecil Howitt, and constructed by local builder, H.W. Pollard. With large crowds of onlookers, the cinema opened under the management of Mr.J.B. Minchington.

1910 Bridgwater Fair
A 'moving pavement' entitled "Nuf Said" was one of the fun features of the annual fair, an amusement owned by Marshall Hills and the lively subject of this photographic postcard taken and published by H.L. Slocombe. The sender of the card appended the interesting message "Thank you for the lovely hat pins".

c. 1908
Was there a third helter skelter for the cameraman to climb that enabled him to take this detailed picture of Bridgwater Fair on a beautiful autumn day? In the distance behind the homes of West Street one can see the masts of the shipping in the docks and just visible between the helter skelter towers is the 110 foot high glass kiln, then within the compound of the Somerset Trading Company in Northgate Road.

1910
J.H. Phillips of 99 St. John Street set up his camera between the tracks of the Bridgwater North Station as the Somerset and Dorset Joint Railway Company's locomotive number 22 returned after an excursion to Blackpool. Behind the engine can be seen the houses in Quantock Terrace, and the signal box is just visible as the last carriage rolls by.

November 20th 1920 Town Hall
Over 400 accepted an invitation to the Kilties Fancy Dress Ball where the first prize winner received £5 and so successful was the event by 7.30p.m. even the balcony was filled. During the evening the pipers played, Miss Mabel Board sang 'The Maid of the Mountains' and music was provided by the orchestra of Mr.E.J. Tout. The grand parade of dancers was led by the Kilties and followed the Highland Fling – and after a wonderful time the festivities were brought to an end at 3.15 the next morning! This photograph by Mr.H.L. Slocombe is of further interest, since it was taken at 12.30a.m. by 'flashlight', a process more appropriate to fireworks than the electronic devices of today.

1922 Eastover School
The playground on Empire Day when, amongst other activities, the pupils, dressed in Sunday best, performed an exhibition netball match before some very proud parents. In the background one can just glimpse the coal trucks of Sully & Co. standing in the railway sidings alongside Rosebery Avenue.

1943
An unusual postcard of a magnificent display mounted by Bridgwater Town Council's Park Department and entitled "Veg for Victory". Obviously a war-time message, perhaps it was an encouragement to other gardeners, akin to the national "Dig for Victory" campaign, to provide a healthy diet and mitigate the effects of food rationing.

1908 High Street
Hours of research have failed to reveal the event shown on this postcard marked July 31st 1908. Crowds had gathered in Penel Orlieu and High Street to watch the gun carriage go by, so magnificently pulled by three pairs of horses and driven by uniformed officers. On the other side of the road in front of Gregory and Vowles Ironmongers, stands a young girl in the back of a cart at the front of which clearly can be seen a milk churn. Does anyone have details of this event?

1911 Coronation
There was rejoicing in the streets of Bridgwater in celebration of the Coronation of King George V with flags and bunting everywhere! Approaching the Cornhill from Fore Street is one of the procession floats as it slowly wended its way through the masses. Apart from best clothes for the occasion, many of the ladies had new or specially trimmed hats, the wide brims affording some protection from the sun on this hot summer's day, as well as marking the importance of the event.

PICTURED FOR THE RECORD

August 6th 1910
Wood & Son photographers of 20 Cornhill were commissioned to commemorate the gathering of one hundred and twenty juveniles and adults celebrating the centenary year of the Independent Order of Oddfellows Manchester Unity at Quantock Farm, Enmore. Exactly what form the celebrations took at the farm is not known, but everyone appears to be very properly dressed!

c. 1906
Although only a pair is shown, four horses pulled this wagonette belonging to the Railway Hotel Bridgwater at a time when Mr. H. Read was the proprietor.

c. 1936
A warm sunny day for the outing of this casually attired group of gentlemen posed in front of one of Fursland's luxury buses, its sun roof folded back for natural air conditioning! Unfortunately no one thought of recording the exact date, the event or the identity of the group.

1924
Thankfully many photographic postcards remain of Bridgwater carnival gangs over the years, but unfortunately few record the date, the name of the gang and the title of the scene portrayed. All that is known from this card is that the scene was entitled 'The Rose of Persia'.

c. 1930
The steps of the now demolished Railway Hotel provide an appropriate venue for this mock marriage group photographed by Mr. S.W. Palfrey, and recording a comic carnival feature entitled 'One Legged Wedding' and entered by the Crown Inn, St. John Street.

c. 1930
Another carnival gang, but the only fact known is the location at the top of St. John Street, the Railway Hotel being just visible in the top right hand corner.

November 1920
In August 1920 a few members from the jazz band of the previous year's carnival got together and with around forty veterans of the 1914-1918 war, formed the Kilties. In Stuart tartan Highland dress and tam-o-shanters decorated with ostrich feathers, around sixty members processed and here posed for an appropriate photograph with their leader, Captain W.H.E. Lockyer, at the time of the November carnival.

c. 1930
A mystery picture. Although the subject matter of this carnival group is not known, clearly they were prizewinners as they gather together for this picture by Mr.S.W. Palfrey, believed to have been taken in the council yard behind the Town Hall. The visual evidence suggests that this occasion may have been a hospital tombola.

c. 1930
Another carnival gang, believed to be that from the Crown Inn, St. John Street and simulating a scene on the R.M.S. Queen Mary.

c.1914
The cavalry of the West Somerset Yeomanry mobilising outside the Masons Arms in Market Street, the signboard of the public house having been blacked out on the negative of the photograph as a precaution and safety measure to avoid identification of the location. The horse trough, then so necessary, is no more. The wall to the left fronted the cattle market, later the site of the Odeon cinema car park, and now a roadway.

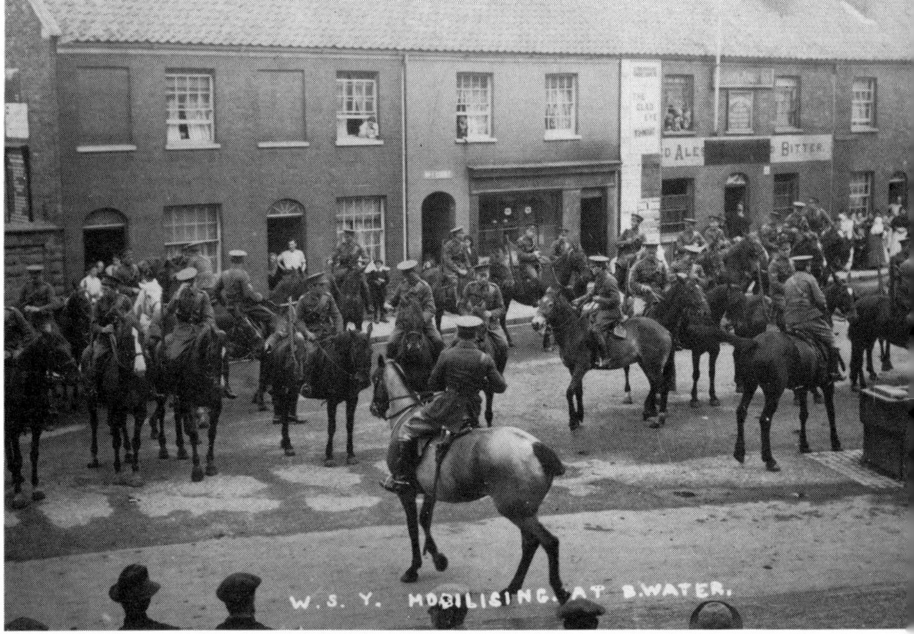

c.1914
The platform of the Somerset and Dorset Railway Station at Bridgwater as a crowd of young men, some uniformed, await the trains's arrival. Was Mr.J. Slocombe photographer of Valetta Place recording the departure from the town of enlisted men en route for the trenches?

c.1914
Another Slocombe view of the station, this time the Great Western Railway platform, and showing some very serious and solemn faced young women and sad looking men of an older generation, perhaps present to wave a tearful farewell to sons and loved ones, some of whom were not destined to return.

c. 1915
In common with many other towns, Bridgwater opened its doors and hearts to refugees without any state financial support who sought the safety of this country following the invasion of Belgium. To provide for the welfare and maintenance of these poor folk, residents of Bridgwater collected money and pictured here is a group of costumed townsfolk in Taunton Road near St. Mary Street with boxes and hand-cart at the ready as their collecting day began.

c. 1915
Some of the Belgian refugees who found temporary shelter in Wembdon.

c. 1928
The founder members of the Bridgwater branch of the British Legion pictured outside Dr. Morgan's school in Mount Street where meetings were held until 1937 when the new school in Durleigh Road was completed. This portrait-style postcard was published by Mr. S.W. Palfrey, and from a variety of sources it is thought the group includes Billy Tamlyn, Auctioneer, D.S. Watson, Solicitor, P. Huggins, H. Burge, Verger of St. Mary's Church, A.Wevell, F. Poad, B. Escott, S.W. Palfrey, B. Bevan, W. Slocombe, the Reverend S. Berry, B. Byers, H. Haggett, Mr. Woodward, Mr. Beechey and W. Barnett. Billy Tamlyn is described as having "served in the Kaiser's war, was a Major and a cheerful popular man" and Solicitor Mr. Watson as "having a practice in Castle Street and a booming voice". The Reverend Seymour Berry was well loved in the town, but died tragically, trying to save his drowning daughter in Cornwall in 1930.

1922
Empire Day and the younger pupils of Eastover school happily enjoy their appearance as cats and kittens.

c. 1933
It was the daughter of the late Mr. S.W. Palfrey who identified this photographic postcard produced by her father and recording the pageant "Wembdon through the Ages" at the town hall. Here the pupils of Grove House School (later Wemdon High School) dutifully posed – with Miss Palfrey herself as a jockey, front right.

Squibbs and Carey, *Photo*

HAVE
SQUIBBS & CAREY
PHOTOGRAPHED
YOU ?

If not, they are waiting for you to call
. . at . .
38, FORE STREET, BRIDGWATER.

c. 1922
A happy record of a successful ten day campaign in Bridgwater by cadets from the national Salvation Army training college, here posed outside the Citadel in Friarn Street.

1908
An interior view of St. John's Church when it was so beautifully decorated for the Harvest Festival, the sheaf of wheat in the foreground traditionally made in bread.

1924
Although not black edged, this photographic postcard was issued following the death of Flag Carrier 'Dad' Paddon, a well known and zealous Salvation Army veteran, and a member of the local corps for over forty years. He died in his home in Chilton Street on 15th June 1924, and his funeral was accorded full Salvation Army honours, the cortège proceeding from the Friarn Street Army Hall to the cemetery in Bristol Road, accompanied by the senior and young people's bands and the Songster Brigade. The following Sunday, a slow march from the town bridge to Friarn Street preceded a memorial service for this loved and respected 84 year old Salvationist.

Eastover Boys School *1924-1925*
From left to right
Top Row
W. Davey, H. Shapter, D. Boyce, A. Manley, W. French, J. Haines, A. Chubb, C. Bird, R. Reakes.
Second Row
S. Dibble, R. Loxton, G. Alsbury, C. Wilkins, L. Gibbs, A. Bartlett, H. Holman, S. Baker, C. Salter, C. Reed.
Third Row
D. Mitchell, H. Griffiths, H. Baker, G. Hawkins, D. Marks, C. Bellringer, R. Thicker, J. Martin, P. Jarvis, L. Payne, W. Evis.
Front Row
C. Bond, H. Newton, J. Bale, H. Rossiter, L. Nelson, J. Harden, R. Temblett, H. Spraggs, E. Young.

Eastover Boys School *September 1924*
Top Row
A. Richards, H. Hawkins, A. Broom, L. Palmer, C. Innalls, F. White, V. Case, W. Smith, E. Jones.
Second Row
H. King, L. Collard, J. Manchip, W. Fowler, F. White, H. Bell, B. Hole, R. Shapter, R. Binding.
Third Row
H. Greedy, L. Knight, W. Luxton, C. Pither, E. French, C. Bennet, H. Prescott, E. Cattle, W. Hallett, H. Parsons, L. Burton.
Fourth Row
S. Buttle, H. Fry, F. Boyce, H. Blackmore, D. Martin, L. Rees, F. Hockey, C. Goddard, H. Burbidge.
Front Row
F. Gardiner, S. Scribbens, F. Cox, C. Paddick, W. Merriott, B. Northover, D. Cooksley, W.Hill, H. Villis, H. Cross.

Eastover Boys School *1921*
Top Row
(Teacher) D. Venning,..Puddy, H. Davis, L. Moule, R. Payne, W. Worman (Teacher).
Middle Row
..Smith, ..French, ..Owens, ..Andrews, F. Turner, ..Buttle,..Fackrell, ..Rossiter, ..Hall.
Front Row
..Jones, ..Chidgey, ..Crouch, ..Cresswell.

1911
Eastover Public Elementary School with pupils and staff in a typical school photograph, this one taken in March 1911.

Produced perhaps for canvassing purposes, these two posed photographic postcards show Mr. H.G. Montgomery, Liberal, and Member of Parliament for the Bridgwater Division of the County of Somerset 1906-1909, and Mr. R.A. Sanders, Conservative and Unionist, and Member of Parliament for the Bridgwater Division of Somerset 1910-1922

1925/6
Eastover Old Boys Football Club team pictured at the rear of the Lime Kiln public house. Happily someone recorded the players:
Back row L. to R. Symonds, Stan Crocker, Whitehead, S. Allen, Fudge.
Middle row L. to R. Franklin, Mansfield, Stan Westcott, Stan Betty, Frank Crocker (Capt.)
Sitting 'Dodger' Venning.

c. 1935
The same Club, but another team recorded on the back as
Back Row L. to R.Goddard, R. Acland, T. Hurford, Cyril Bott, Ron Gillespie, Purse Moore, Allen.
Front Row L. to r. Vince Goddard, Lou Fossil, Frank Crocker (Capt) Morris Hawkins, Harry Phillips, Freddie Scott.

Frank Crocker, one of the players pictured, kindly provided these two cards, for which the authors are grateful and happy to acknowledge

c. 1935 Albert Street School
Two photographs, both apparently taken around the same time by Mr. S.W. Palfrey, and showing rows of well scrubbed little boys and their teachers. Sadly no-one recorded any names, but perhaps someone may be able to identify some of these angelic juniors!

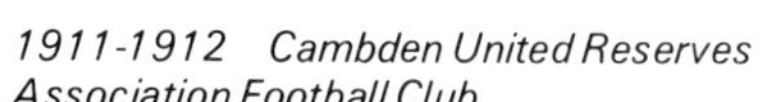

1911-1912 Cambden United Reserves Association Football Club
The players and linesmen of the team proudly posed in the studio of Mr. H.L. Slocombe. Despite research, enquiries to date have failed to reveal the origin and history of this club, perhaps based on Cambden Road.

c. 1932
Another postcard by Mr. S.W. Palfrey, this time believed to show members of the Bridgwater Comrades Club celebrating success in winning a major darts trophy. The club was started in 1920 and had premises in St. Mary Street. The reverse of the card identifies some of those shown as Harry Burge, Albert Lock, Harry Beavan, Mr. Bloodworth and Mr. Hayward.

c. 1908
No doubt a family photograph of the son of the household at 38 Barclay Street, a property later demolished to make way for the Broadway relief road. In many instances, photographs were processed and printed for the customer in postcard form, and if readers have a look at their old family albums it may be surprising how many photographic postcards will be found.

c. 1908
A young sportsman poses in the studio of Mr. H.L. Slocombe, a portrait photographic postcard undoubtedly commissioned by parents proud of their son in hunting attire with rabbit and gun, indeed the family may well have been local landowners, who knows?

1908
A pair of beautifully groomed horses pulled this elaborate hearse with its elegantly attired coachmen for Gilberts, local undertakers, of St. John Street. This photographic postcard by J. Phillips of 99 St. John Street is indeed a record of local social history.

c. 1907
The horse and cart of 'Gramp' Warren pictured in the brickyard of H.J. Major & Co. Ltd., in Colley Lane.

1931
At first sight this card is an oddity until turned over, for there the sender carefully affixed a newspaper cutting from June 1931 headed "A strange phenomenon-Remarkable growth in Bridgwater skittle alley". The alley belonged to Mr. White, the landlord of the Lime Kiln Inn, Salmon Parade and in the construction of an extension, an ash tree was felled. From time to time fungi had been seen growing on the site of the tree stump, but in June 1931 the growths resembling coral branches and ivory water lillies assumed gigantic proportions, attracting crowds of interested observers from near and far. Not even a local expert on fungi could identify the genus of these strange growths or explain their appearance, but Mr. White took advantage of the atrraction and placed nearby a box in which sightseers could leave a donation in aid of the hospital, and had photographs taken which he sold "at a nominal charge". Undoubtedly this postcard was one of them

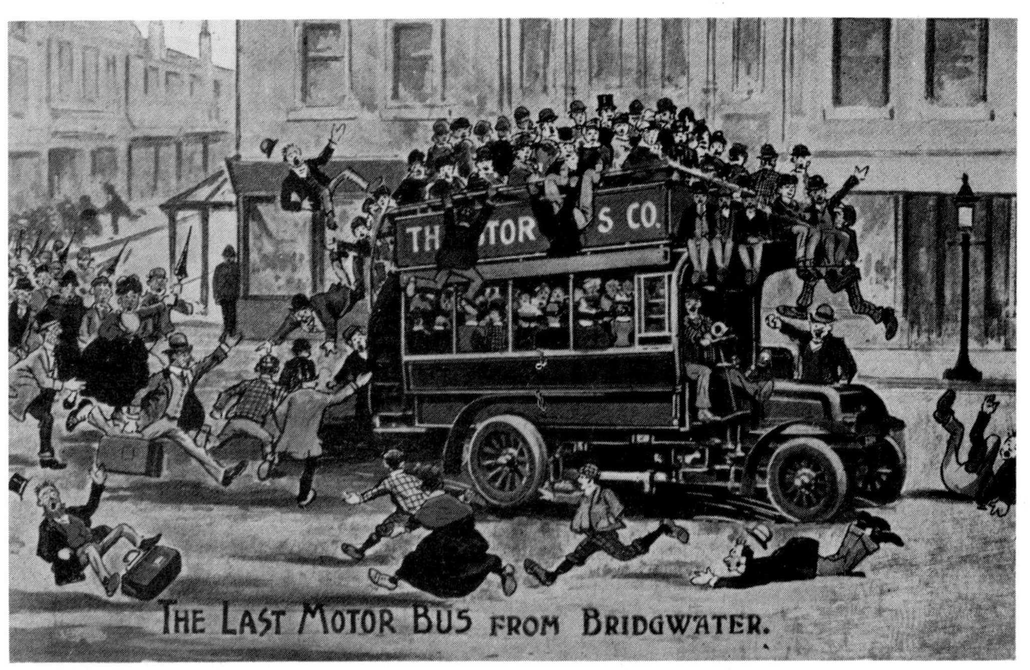

Comic cards are fun and laughter,
Just a joke for years thereafter,
Showing fashion, loves divine,
Revealing humour, time to time.

C.F.

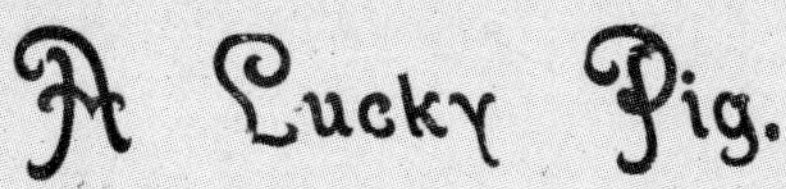

You may push me
You may shuv
But I'm hanged
If I'll be druv
From BRIDGWATER.

THE RIVER, DOCKS & WATERWAYS

c. 1906
From the corner of Fore Street and Binford Place and looking towards Carvers dry dock and the 'Black Bridge', this postcard captures the sight of the busy wharfs over eighty years ago. Alongside East Quay is the ketch 'Good Templar' built in Goole Yorkshire in 1881, which foundered in 1911. Behind the ketch at 6/7 East Quay are the premises of Wilkinson and Leng Ltd., an old established firm of builders merchants

1912
The ketch 'Emma', here seen with drying sails draped over the bowsprit, with the town bridge visible through the rigging. This particular boat was built at Pill in 1865 and sank in 1917.

c.1912
Double-ended Parrett barges carrying bricks and tiles and plying between Bridgwater and the upper reaches of the river were moored frequently alongside the quay at Binford Place. The barge to the left was owned by Colthurst Symons, whose brickyard at Castle Field works produced the famous 'Bath' brick.

c. 1905
The ketch 'Eliza', built at Runcorn in 1865 and broken up in 1949, pictured here unloading alongside East Quay. Across the river is the old Anchor Inn, a familiar haunt of sailors and seamen, closing its doors in 1907 and subsequently demolished.

The Quays, Bridgwater.

— This View shows the Factory of —
WILKINSON & LENG, Ltd., Builders' Merchants, Slate, Cement & Hardware Dealers, Bridge Works, Bridgwater.

c. 1905
The ketch 'Good Intent', built in 1790 at Plymouth and used regularly until 1920, when she ran aground in Bristol when 130 years old. She is seen here moored opposite the dry dock entrance with the old established firm of Peace Ltd., removal contractors, shipping and insurance agents to the right, a company with premises at West Quay and Chandos Street and running its own steamers out of Bristol and Cardiff.

35082
The Quay, Bridgwater

c. 1905
The docks with the dredger 'Bertha' belonging to the Great Western Railway Company in the foreground. Constructed in 1844, she was in continuous use until the docks closed in 1971. Behind 'Bertha' are moored three ketches, that nearest the camera being the 1873 Harwich-built 'Crowpill', registered in Bridgwater, which gave sterling service until it ran aground in 1913. Ware's warehouse in the background was built in 1841 with three bays and around 1870 extended to five bays. Completing this historic record is the 110 foot high glass kiln, built as far back as 1734 at the expense of the Duke of Chandos and not demolished until 1943. Thankfully the foundations remained and more recently have been restored amidst the redevelopment of the area generally and with an explanatory plaque preserved for posterity and the education of those who might otherwise live in ignorance of the town's industrial heritage.

c. 1904
Many ships, but no movement, perhaps a tranquil Sunday because even the two fellows in the foreground appear attired in best clothes! To the left is the ketch 'Crowpill' and moored alongside is the 1873 Ipswich-built ketch 'Parkend' which ran aground in 1917. To the right is the 'Circe' with the square rigged 'Marie Eugenie' moored astern, a schooner built in Regneville and broken up in 1927.

c. 1904
This artistic study of the inner basin with Ware's warehouse framed by the masts and chimneys of sail and steam vessels was produced by Page & Son of 42 Fore Street.

c. 1920
The tidal dock basin, looking towards the dock-master's house, viewed from the bascule bridge. The third boat to the right is the Bridgwater-built steam collier 'Tender', built in 1874 for Sully & Co. and not broken up until 1943.

c. 1935
The floating dock or inner basin, looking east towards the Holms sand and gravel wharf with the premises of British Oil and Cake Mills to the right. On the left is the Chester-registered ketch 'North Barrjle'.

c. 1903
Few strangers to the area would believe that this rural view of the canal, looking east from the towpath, was so close to the heart of busy Bridgwater, but this bridge carries the now busy Taunton Road over the canal.

1912
The 'Black Bridge' as the telescopic bridge was known locally. Built in 1871 at a cost of £8000, it has remained a landmark ever since and, recently restored, is now preserved as a foot-bridge amidst the exciting development around the docks. The building alongside contained the steam engine that controlled the traverse section of the bridge, which when moved sideways, made room for the centre bridge section to be rolled back in its place.

1912
The footpath alongside the river at Saltlands on one of the series of thirty cards produced by Judges following the 1912 visit to Bridgwater by its photographers.

1917
January 1917 and a severe winter caused ice floes to form on the Parrett. Mr. J. Slocombe from his studio in Valletta Place only had to walk a few yards to take this unusual view of the frozen river.

ASHCOTT

c. 1905
This building still stands, although few people travelling the road from Ashcott to Meare today would recognise immediately the present house as the former Ashcott railway station on the Somerset and Dorset line, but for those who stop and look closer, all is revealed. Two of the level crossing gateposts with their original hinges still stand, and a glance to each side of the road reveals where the railway lines ran. Matching a turn of the century postcard with the location is all part of the fun of deltiology.

c. 1905
Pipers Inn with Slocombes Pipers Inn bakery and refreshment rooms, the horse-pulled cart belonging to the bakery and used for delivering bread. Frank Slocombe, the owner, also had other property at 173 High Street, Street.

ATHELNEY

c. 1907
On the Willow Craft trail, with a view taken from the north side of the road, looking towards the railway level crossing. The white-fronted house in the foreground no longer stands, but behind it is Myrtle Tree House, now owned and occupied by Mr. and Mrs. Witchell, happy on a Sunday October afternoon to stand and talk about their home which has passed down from one generation to another from within the family from Dampier (a Somerset surname of famous origins) to Hembrow and now Witchell. Discovering the origins and finding the location of a postcard scene has proved a pleasurable way of making new friends, and it was gratifying to be reassured that the history of Athelney still remains of great interest to residents. Although this card is titled 'Stanmore', residents maintain that the properties are in Athleney, Stanmore being the area of road and property before one gets to this point.

1905
This photograph was taken from the level crossing looking south, with an elderly lady attired in dress more appropriate to some thirty years earlier. Was it Nellie Francis, Grace Boyland, or someone else? Behind her is the now chimney-less cider house of Bill Becks and other houses externally little changed over the years, some with evocative names like 'Windy Willows' and 'Timbuktu'. Apart from the cider house, it is the sheds on the left that are of particular interest, originally built for the storage and drying of withies before use in the customary crafts. Some of the sheds are used now for storage of a different sort and more in the nature of garages! This card is titled Athelney, but is the stretch of road known as Curload, as is also the card of the floods, on 1918 maps referred to as Curry Load.

c. 1929
The floods of 1929 at a point known as the Sheilings, according to local people. Interestingly one even now can find the point at which it seems this photograph was taken, and given the position of the houses on the banks of the River Tone and the flat lands beyond, it is easy to imagine what it was like when the banks burst and flooded the area.

1905
Cards and research suggest two signal boxes. Athelney and Athelney West and that the Station Master was Henry. B, Salter.This card of Athelney signal box, sadly bears no other information, and one wonders who the two men were standing between the tracks (thankfully the gates were closed).

BAWDRIP

c. 1930
Stopping in the village one morning with a tentative enquiry of a lady in the Churchyard, fortuitously she proved to be Miss 'Cissy' Gilbert who had spent years at the local school helping in a variety of ways and who proved to be so informative. She identified the happy faces as the pupils of Bawdrip Council School taking part in the 1930 Christmas Concert and thought that some of the youngsters were:
Back row 1st left-Arthur March; the tall veiled girl Peggy Gilbert; front row 3rd left-Sellick; 4th -Crane; 5th- Emily Sellick; 6th- Joyce Sellick; far right Derek Collinson. Whoever they were, they look as though they were enjoying themselves.

BURTLE

c. 1912
Mr. Vowles, photographer of Minehead, completed a series of postcard views showing life on the Somerset levels. Here he has captured a familiar event as a farmer punts his boat across the flooded moor near Burtle to collect hay for the cattle up on the higher ground.

BURTON

c. 1930
The local smith following his trade outside his workshop, a familiar sight in country districts then, but rarely so these days. The site of the workshop is not difficult to find, now part of a private house in the village and surrounded neatly with white-painted stones.

BURROWBRIDGE

c. 1912
The building on the extreme right now with delapidated roof is derelict, the flat-roofed property has gone and only a telephone booth occupies the site. That building in fact was the toll house where a fee was paid before the gates over the road were opened and passage over the bridge then allowed. The discontinuance of tolls led to the removal of the gates and then no further need for a tollhouse keeper. The cart on the left is very typical of local design. At the time these photographs of Burrowbridge were taken, the sight of a photographer was rare and therefore a big event especially attracting children anxious to become part of the picture. Who were these children, does anyone know?

c. 1906
The other side of the tollhouse, looking towards Othery and from the message on the reverse of the card it is obvious that the family pictured here comprised the tollkeeper, his wife, child and dog! The signboard on the side of the tollhouse sets out all the relevant dues payable as tolls. The right to use public roads free of tolls was a political issue, but how interesting is that all these years later tolls have been re-introduced in some places and may well become a feature of future travel.

CANNINGTON

c. 1907
These cottages in Bridgwater Road, Cannington remain easily located, even though the grass verge has been incorporated within a widened and now busy road.

c. 1909
The Village hall, then the post office, and in the road some very properly pinafored young ladies pose for the photographer. The volume of traffic these days would make this a scene almost impossible to repeat.

c. 1908
Again a view little changed, including the two telephone poles! Number 18, the first house on the left, is next to Cob Cottage which now has a lowered roof. Beyond number 14 is Ye Olde Willow Tea Rooms with the Kings Head, now embellished with black shutters, at the end of this attractive row of homes.

c. 1910
Cannington brook in flood, undoubtedly an event to be recorded in the days before radio and television and when few homes had a telephone. Photographic cards therefore had more than one use, preserving memorable events as well as being a means of communication.

CATCOTT

c. 1908
A mid-day view of Manor Road with the post office to the right in the distance and Ben's Cottage next to Vine Cottage in the foreground. Was the gentleman carrying home madam's shopping, but obliged to wait whilst she passed the time of day with a neighbour?

c. 1921
The junction of Brook Lane to the left with Manor Road to the right and a superb setting for the war memorial. Although these cottages have been modernised, faced and colour washed, only telephone wires and poles now change this view.

CHEDZOY

c. 1906
Front Street with the village hall to the right. Only a tarmacadam surface, pavements and kerb stones, and of course the traffic, appear to have changed this scene substantially from the days when a farmer could shepherd his flock of sheep down the main street, and still find time to stand and chat!

COMBWICH

c. 1905
In the creek shown here at low tide, boats would bring in cargoes of coal, and in exchange take out bricks and tiles made locally. A number of craft were Combwich owned, the last being the Emily, which belonged to the Farmers Association. This particular card was published by Combwich photographer Mr. H. Frear and, from the banks and moorage of the boat, shows the extent of the rise and fall of the tide.

COSSINGTON

c. 1910
A rutted dirt road, now a blaze of dotted white and yellow zig zag lines and a proliferation of road signs, the spoliation of the rural scene necessary on grounds of safety for the benefit of the children attending Cossington County primary school and using the small pillared entrance to the right.

c. 1907
Was this a card of romance from one of the haymaking chaps, sent to the lady of his heart? The evidence is the stamp on the other side of the card, stuck on at an angle to the corner, the secret sign of a kiss, coupled with the omission of any message – just the address, Miss E. Salisbury, Manor Dairy, Cossington, and suggesting perhaps that the picture and the kiss were enough.....? The card was sent on August 7th 1907 and any other information would be most welcome.

DUNBALL

c. 1904
The wharf, opened in 1843 and in constant use ever since, providing sail, steam and now modern freight shipping with facilities for loading and unloading.

c. 1904
An interesting scene, looking from the wharf with the Dunball Railway station on the main Bridgwater to Bristol GWR line. The level crossing gates at times of train arrivals closed the roads in and out of the quarries and stoneworks of John Board and Company, established since 1844. Few other local enterprises had such easy access to and from road, rail and wharf. The company of John Board manufactured Portland cement, hydraulic blue lime, plaster of Paris, patent tiles, bricks, drain pipes, pottery and patent bath scouring bricks.

DURSTON

c. 1907
A country lane, but now the widened and very busy A 361 and where no one would be safe standing in the middle of the road in daylight, either as a photographer or subject! Not much effort was needed to locate the scene, although it would seem that this end of the thatched cottage up to the chimney has been demolished. Behind the man in the middle of the road is Warrs Farmhouse. The properties and the owners , as well as the man pictured here, must have a tale to tell, but does anyone know the story?

c. 1908.
For our benefit all these years later, Harry writing to "Dear old girl" told Miss Wood of Norwich that "this postcard is a bit of a novelty. Its a photo of the breakdown gang at work clearing up a mess on the rail about 4 miles from here. About 12 trucks went off the line from a heavy goods train last Saturday morning early. Hope the photo will reach you safely. The place is called Durston a junction of two main lines". Thank you Harry!

ENMORE

c. 1907
The Gospel Hall, now the Enmore Chapel, set in the countryside on the Bridgwater side of the village. The building today has an extended porch and more substantial walls, but the corrugated roof remains unchanged, including the distinctively decorated finials.

FIDDINGTON

c. 1913
The post office with its postbox in the left-hand wall of the house. A delightful scene with three children playing behind the cabbage patch on a sunny afternoon whilst their elders look on benignly. Although there is a postbox serving the village today, all efforts to trace the property failed, leading one to question whether it was demolished some time ago?

GOATHURST

c. 1906
The character and appearance of the post office, now Vine Cottage, appears unchanged despite the passage of time. In this quiet lane the children were able to play happily and safely, as they did on the day this photographer passed there way.

HUNTWORTH GATE

c. 1930
A postcard published for Petroil Installations Ltd., of London to advertise its products, using the newly constructed Huntworth Gate as an example of its modern petrol filling stations. The pumps advertise petrol with names well remembered but not now seen, Cleveland, Ethyl and Mercury.

HUNTSPILL

c. 1905
The main A 38 from Bridgwater looking towards Highbridge with what is now the Sundowner Hotel and Restaurant on the left. To the right and in New Road is the county primary school, with the date 1897 over the portals.

c. 1910
A close-up of the frontage to the Ilex Stores where three ladies assisted the owner, Mr. Gilbert J. Burnett, in serving anything from groceries to drapery and 'general items'. This card was published by the same Mr. Burnett as a means of advertising his stock and offering "special value in long cloths, calicoes, sheetings, cotton goods, flannels and flannelettes". This is a good example of a postcard which is equally interesting on both sides.

1913/14
A card that speaks for itself:-
"Huntspill United A.F.C. 1913-1914. Winners of Highbridge League and Knock-out Cups" and listing the players:-
Top row left to right:
E. Cann, H. Hobbs, E. Williams, F. Baldwin F. Brimson, N.J. Reynolds, W. Callaway, The. Reverend C.F. Pizey, F. Woodward, J. Southern, Dr. Mathews, J. Baker, F. Leatheby.
2nd row, left to right:
F. Iley, E. Andrews, S. Coombes, A. Holley (captn.) A. Bond, F. Giles, T. Came (Hon. Sec.)
3rd row, left to right:
A. Palmer, F. Gannicott, W. Palmer F. Inder.

View of Huntspill shewing The Stores.

c. 1904
The main road, this time looking towards Bridgwater, the Ilex Stores now on the right side with the holm oak trees from which, in latin form, the shop took its name.

c. 1903
Another early view of the main road to Highbridge with the 17th century hostelry, known to everyone as the Crossway Inn. The rutted road is self evident of its common usage by horses and horse-drawn vehicles, only adding to the discomfort of those first drivers and passengers of the motor car with its then solid wheels!

c. 1912
The forecourt of the Crossway Inn, but who was the little girl so charmingly astride a pony held by an equally anonymous and even younger little boy?

KNOWLE

c. 1950
Although a somewhat modern postcard, this view of the Silver Fish Café is a valuable addition to a collection as a reminder of what was – and is no more, an example of history in one's own life-time!

LILSTOCK

c. 1908
The Church dedicated to St. Andrew was demolished in 1880, leaving only the mortuary and small bellcote in the walled churchyard. Sadly the chapel is now roofless, the windows broken, and just a shell remains, housing the font and war memorials.

c. 1923
Lilstock Farm, photographed in 1923 and little changed in outward appearance over sixty five years later.

EAST LYNG

c. 1906
An interesting view and a little unusual for the period, having been taken from the Church tower when aerial views were a novelty. Clearly visible to the left is the Rose & Crown which continues to serve customers of the locality, but the houses to the right have been demolished and replaced with a modern development.

c. 1905
A card like this leaves one wondering if the place will ever be located and despite the overprint "View of Lyng" doubts arose as to whether this was a Somerset topographical card or not. Then by chance one afternoon looking for somewhere different, a corner was turned and there it was, the questioned "View of Lyng". The road now is wide and busy, the property no longer in so rural an area, such being the march of so-called progress with housing developments and the like. Nevertheless Laburnum House, or Laburnum Farmhouse with its new front brick wall stands firm as a tribute to its occupants and original builder.

MEARE

16th June 1921
This postcard probably shows the unveiling of the village war memorial at Meare in mid-June 1921, a sad and moving occasion for those present

MIDDLEZOY

c. 1908
An aerial view of Church Road probably taken from the top of the tower of the Church of the Holy Cross. Landmarks remaining include the Wesleyan Methodist Church with its attractive latticed windows, built in 1898, but not surprisingly there has been development, notably in the foreground, with houses in Hollies Close opposite Hollies Farm on the right

c. 1925
A deserted scene of Main Road at the foot of Kicks Hill. It is now a smarter looking number 5, Clematis House that faces the road with number 48, Jones Farm, on the other side of the road.

c. 1910
Miss Mary Elizabeth Crane standing outside the Middlezoy post office where she was the sub-postmistress. She received letters from Bridgwater twice daily at 7.20a.m. and 6.50p.m., six days a week, but in those days it was highly respected position for which only a few were qualified – and the postmaster was even more important!

MOORLYNCH

c. 1905
Greinton Road, Moorlynch, with Collins Farm to the right and East End and Stone Cottage beyond, all seen through the camera of Wood & Son of Chilton Polden. The cottage to the left has long since gone, the site now overgrown and with only an opening where the gate stood to serve as a reminder that a family once lived there.

NETHER STOWEY

c. 1906
An early picture of the stores at the corner of Castle Street and Lime Street, including the Temperance Hotel outside which the horse-drawn cart is pulled up, the driver no doubt performing the service advertised on the cart – "Families Supplied - Daily Whole Meal and Pure White Bread."

c. 1916
A village of distinction and historical and literary significance, remembered by most for the residence there for a while of Samuel Taylor Coleridge, and association with Wordsworth, Southey and Thomas Poole. In this photographic postcard we have moved to the other end of the village with the ancient toll house on the left. Opposite are some interesting buildings, numbers 14,16 and 18 St. Mary Street, now converted into attractive town homes. Next door is Brook House, which in 1916 was the livery stable of James Hobbs, who advertised "Two and four horse brakes, laundaus and wagonettes", and it is outside his business that the beautiful carriage is parked. Further down on the right Mr. A.F. Culliford carried on business as a cycle agent and stockist of Riley Cycles – what memories for those of older years!

c. 1909
The Nether Stowey Womans Club celebrating its 103rd anniversary with a procession through the streets. At three o'clock in the afternoon precisely and led by the Stogursey brass band, the procession started from Lime Street past the George and the Rose & Crown hotel with Miss Sherard carrying the bannerette bearing the words "Forethought and Union linked by Christian Love", the principle on which the Club was founded in 1806. The procession attracted a large crowd of onlookers, and finally ended at the Church by which time a number of local children had 'fallen in' behind the band! By 1907 membership of the Womans Club totalled 81, attracting women from further afield and in the first five months of that year raising £231 reported as being "to the pleasure of the President", Mrs. E.W. Chambers.

NORTH CURRY

c. 1905
Queens Square and a postcard fit for transport history books with the beautiful horse-drawn closed carriage stationary in front of the gas lamp, removed when the 1914-18 war memorial was erected on this junction. Behind the carriage and through the trees is a glimpse of the old brewery at number 19, now a private dwellinghouse with an interesting past, appropriately remembered in the name of the house 'The Old Brewery'.

c. 1912
The premises of Howard Edgar Hearle of Greenway, North Curry, local wheelwright, carpenter and undertaker, pictured here at around the age of thirty years with two of his assistants and a third unknown youngster who came into the picture carrying a cat! For author Rod Fitzhugh this picture is special, for over thirty years later he would sit on Mr. Hearle's knee and watch him drink his tea, not from the cup but the saucer! Howard Edgar Hearle who died in 1948 was his grandfather!

1909
Very prim and proper, the pupils of North Curry public elementry school pose with hardly a smile with headmaster James Alexander Williams, nicknamed by the children "Boss" Williams, standing at their side.

NORTH PETHERTON

c. 1907
A sunny day and the postman drives his horse and cart on the wrong side of Fore Street, perhaps indicating the volume of traffic at the time! Posed proudly outside his establishment, Manchester House on the corner of Clare Street, is the proprietor Mr. Albert Scott, draper and outfitter. The present proprietor, W.C. Gibbs, continues to cater for like needs, advertising specialities as 'Draper-Carpeting – Outfitters-Footwear'. It was as the result of contact with the authors by Mr. P. Druce of North Petherton that this card appears, and to him they are most grateful.

c. 1918
Fore Street, the local lads pictured with the familiar 'sit up and beg' style bicycles of the day. The youth to the left held his cycle in full view of the camera, hoping no doubt to publicise the notice below the crossbar, 'S. Gadd, Steam Bakery, North Petherton' and true enough in his front basket are the loaves freshly baked by Samuel Gadd of Fore Street, due for delivery. Behind him is the 'George Hotel-Motor Garage'. The building in the right foreground has given way to the drive-in for the Walnut Tree Inn.

1911
The Coronation Arch erected for the celebrations of 22nd June. Lower down the road at the other end of the town was another arch across the road, bearing the words 'God Save Our King and Queen' a postcard of which appeared in the authors' first book. The United Reformed Church to the right of the arch was built in 1833 as the Congregational Church, rebuilt in 1869, and in part dedicated later as a memorial to those who served and fell in the Great War and with some rebuilding again in 1922.

1908
Perhaps more by accident than design but a British 'Bobby' with watchful eye accompanies a sedate procession by members of the congregation of the Church of St. Mary down Fore Street. All attired in Sunday best, this photographic record is worthy of a place in a costume museum. The card was posted on 23rd December 1908 by M.L. Heywood to Miss M. Davis in Weston-Super-Mare "wishing you all a very happy and merry Christmas and a bright and prosperous New Year". The picture postcard had many uses!

c. 1909
A very rare card and incredibly clear, a credit to whoever cared for it over the years, it features the 'corn factors, grocers, bakers, confectioners and glass and china depot' of T. Warren & Son on the corner of Fore Street and School Lane. Sent by 'Elsie', she refers to "our shop" and records confirm that at least between 1897 and 1935 the premises were kept by successive members of the Warren family. Presently called 'Four Bees', the shop still advertises fresh bread and cakes as well as fruit and vegetables, its external appearance little changed.

c. 1910
A bleak scene obviously on a cold day, given the overcoat of the cyclist on the A 38 a short distance from where the modern Huntworth island leads up to the M5, but in the years when it was a lonely stretch known to pedestrians, horse-drawn carts, the occasional cyclist and only very rarely one of those 'new fangled contraptions' – the horseless carriage or motor car. What a difference today!

July 1908
Scenes from the 'Old English Fair' held to raise funds for the Congregational Church, at that time the only local Free Church with a resident Minister, and then having a membership of over one hundred. The fund target was £400, a modest sum today, but of far greater value then and sufficient to pay for a new heating system, floor renewals, other renovations, Church events and make donations to Christian Endeavour, Boys' Brigade, Men's Own and Woman's Meeting. From an orchard opposite the Church, the fête attracted crowds anxious to see the full-scale replicas of old English shops. These included one in Georgian style displaying wood-work, a Jacobean shop with plain needlework, a Queen Anne-style construction with a miscellaneous assortment of goods arranged by the Mens Own group, and yet another also in Georgian style selling sweets and fruit, and with welcome refreshments dispensed from the Elizabethan style shop. This 'Old English Fair' was far from flimsy, for each building was constructed with stonework, tiling and solignum. More especially each 'shop' was built in strict accordance with plans prepared by Mr. F.H.J. Gabbutt, a Bridgwater architect, and derived even greater permanency from lighting provided by a system of gas acetylene. Every shop assistant was attired in period costume and each evening the fair was illuminated with lights in the trees with an additional 4000 candle power from flares providing an appropriate background for the grand lantern tattoo.

NORTH NEWTON

1910
The only lead on identifying this card was the postmark, not always much help, but in the village luckily, the first person asked was local farmer, Mr. Sellick, who quickly identified the photograph as the rear of Masey's, the village butcher, where cattle and sheep were slaughtered on the premises, now called 'Penrod', a private house. Mr. Sellick kindly pointed out not just the property but the position of the original and now bricked-up shop door. Thanks to Mr. Sellick another mystery was solved, and now even the message on the back makes sense. Sent "From Yours Forever.E.R." in North Newton to Miss Bessie Masey, c/o Mr. C. Masey, All Round Dealer, Flaxpool Farm, Crocombe it requested "continued friendship" and "I hope you will forgive me for last Sunday". Again the stamp was affixed at an angle to the corner, the means of sending a kiss – so was this some secret romance between the unidentified E.R. and Bessie Masey?

OTHERY

c. 1912
A country road with its earth surface rutted from waggons and carts, its then regular traffic. Laburnum Cottage, set back from the road and opposite Bedwell Lane, is easy to find today on this busy A 361. The smaller house on the kerb edge called The Cottage is next to the 1883 brick-built extension to the Congregational Chapel, itself constructed of red stone in 1836, next to Garfield House.

c. 1908
The public elementary school built in 1880 for the education of 120 children, but with records showing an average attendance of 70; undoubtedly the rest being engaged in working the family farms rather than deliberately truanting to play!

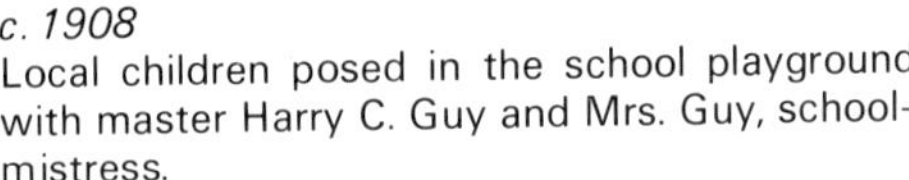

c. 1908
Local children posed in the school playground with master Harry C. Guy and Mrs. Guy, schoolmistress.

The Church, Othery.

c. 1912
The fourteenth century Church of St. Michael, seating 400, with its 75 foot high tower and five bells, a truly magnificent Church for a small area, and denoting the importance of the locality at the time it was built. The thatched cottage is no more, and new buildings have replaced the farm buildings opposite.

OVER STOWEY

2nd October 1907
St. Peter and St. Paul Parish Church, Over Stowey and the funeral of Mr. Edward James Stanley, who died at his home at Quantock Lodge at 2.40a.m. on Saturday September 28th 1907, aged 81 years. Born in Crosslin, Lancashire in 1826, he is remembered as the faithful Member of Parliament for the Bridgwater division from 1884 to 1906 when he retired. Mr. Stanley was loved by many for his devotion to the needs of his constituents, and not suprisingly, his death was seen as a big loss not only to the area but to his party which he had served for so long. His funeral therefore was an occasion attended by many, anxious to pay their last respects and give thanks for his work. At 2p.m. the cortège left Quantock House led by the male staff, arriving in the village at 2.45p.m. when it was met at the Church gates by the Bishop of Bath and Wells, and other clergy including Dr. Powell, Vicar and Rural Dean of Bridgwater, and a well known author of superb reference books on the ancient borough of Bridgwater. After an inspiring service Mr. Stanley was laid to rest in the family vault in the Church, alongside Lord and Lady Taunton, the late parents of his widow, the Honourable Mrs Mary Dorothy Stanley.

PAWLETT

c. 1908
The old main road between Bridgwater and Highbridge before the village was bypassed. On the corner of Gaunts Road is the post office and stores, still serving the village in that way today, although the shop has been moved back, the shop front shown here now forming part of the residential accommodation. In 1908 or thereabouts when this photograph was taken, the Pawlett Stores under the proprietorship of Mr. W.R. Squance was advertising 'Tea at 1d a cup' and 'Refreshments for cyclists'.

c. 1935
The main A 38 Bridgwater to Pawlett road, as a solitary motor car travels towards the town. This picture was taken by Charles Pearson of Burnham-on-Sea, a man now recognised as one of the finest local postcard photographers of the district. On his bicycle, he covered a large area from the Quantocks to the Mendips but surprisingly he never set up his camera in Bridgwater.

PURITON

c. 1908
The Congregational Chapel, built in 1872 and rebuilt of stone in 1904, is now a private house. Although modified by the setting back of the second gable to provide a driveway, externally it retains the ecclesiastical appearance of the building. Not even the two ridge tiles missing at the time of this picture have been replaced, perhaps because of their unusual design.

c. 1907
The imposing and somewhat Gothic-style entrance and elaborate wrought iron gates to Puriton Manor, itself of more modern vintage. On the junction of Rye, Middle Street and Woolavington Road, the house at the time was occupied by lord of the manor, Christopher William Moore Greenhill.

c. 1908
The quarries of John Board & Company from where the stone for cement and lime was excavated.

SHAPWICK

c. 1907
Swayne's Leap in Loxley Wood on the main road between Bridgwater and Glastonbury and on the hill-top between Shapwick and Moorlynch. The famous 'Leaps' commemorate an event after the Battle of Sedgemoor when a captured soldier named Swayne with his legs bound together, was then "encouraged" to try and escape, giving his Royalist captors an excuse to shoot him. However, the man was so strong that he made three sudden leaps of great distance and disappeared into the woods, thereby saving his life. His giant leaps are now marked by the stones shown here.

SPAXTON

c. 1907
Unused now, but it would be a sad loss if the old blacksmith's shop was not preserved. In this picture the smithy is seen with four local lads, who by their stance appear to have been purposely posed by the photographer to lend charm to the picture, although the younger child standing alone appears to have wandered into the scene unintentionally and to be merely curious as any child would be of such goings on!

c. 1909
Wayside Cottage in High Street next to the village pump, presumably erected in Queen Victoria's Diamond Jubilee year, since it bears the dates 1837-97. Stowey Cottage and the properties beyond lead into Pightly Road.

STOGURSEY

1920
On 19th April 1920 the tribute to the fallen of the Great War 1914-18 was unveiled in the village at a spot known as 'The Gravel'. Standing eighteen feet high and carved from Doulton stone, the Cross by Tapper of London was surmounted by a Crucifix on one side and the Blessed Virgin Mary on the reverse with a representation of St. Andrew, patron Saint of the Parish Church, on the base. A total of £260 had been raised locally for the erection of this memorial to the twenty four villagers who gave of their lives in the service of the nation and in the cause of freedom.
The inscription reads "Jesu, Mercy, Pray for the Souls of A. Binding, M. Binding, G. Bushell, S Chilcott, T. Chilcott, C. Crowcombe, B. Gunningham, G, Gunningham, S. Gunningham, E. Harrison, E. Howe, C. Jones, A. Kable, H. Kennedy, A. Millard, A. Payne, G. Payne, H. Perry, R. Ridler-Rowe, R. Rymer, R. Scott, W. Scott, G. Smith, A. Taylor, M.D.C.C.C.C. XIX". Somerset sons, the souls of whom should never be forgotten, joining those who gave yeomen service through the centuries.

c. 1904
An early scene in the High Street by that much travelled photographer Montague Cooper, with the familiar crowd of children that always seemed to gather whenever the tripod, camera and covering black cloth were set up.

STOKE ST. GREGORY

c. 1909
Subsequent to this photograph, the post office was moved elsewhere and the building reverted to a private house. Directly opposite stand the Baptist Church and adjoining manse with Chapel House in the distance.

c. 1905
A view down Curload Hill on a winter's day, with the village 'bobby' and an unidentified, elegantly attired gentlewoman lending character to an otherwise cheerless view.

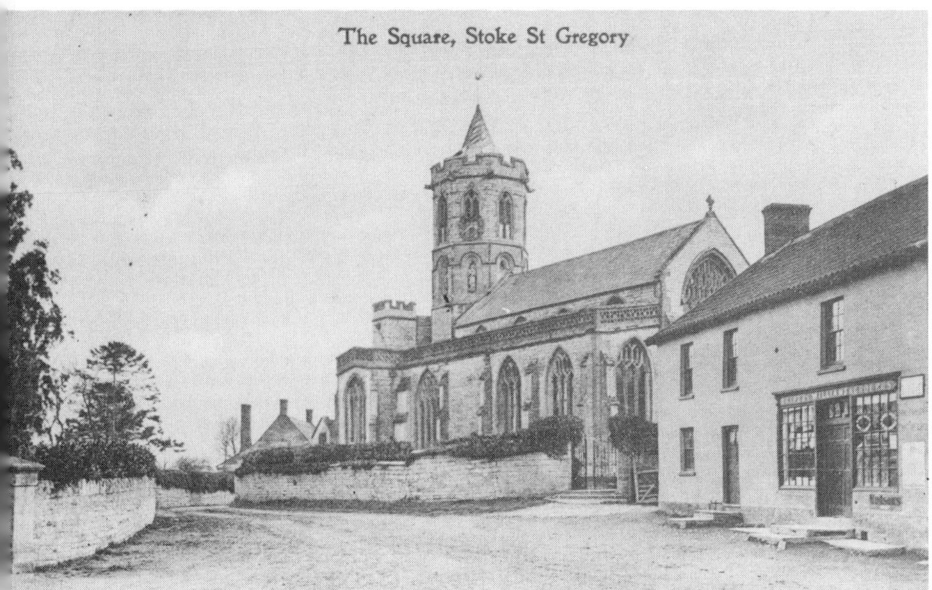

c. 1907
The magnificence of Stoke St. Gregory's Church next to the village shop of Williams, drapers and grocers, and opposite Stoke House on the corner of Dark Lane. Together they form The Square, little changed in outward appearance by the intervening years.

STAWELL

c. 1930
The posts and chain no longer appear in front of number 8 the Manor House, with its ornate stone pillars and next to Manor Farm with the fancy roof. A telephone box now intrudes on the scene, a modern need in a village which appears to have weathered the storm of change and to be little different despite the intervening decades. Although not quite so immense these days, a leaning tree continues to flourish in the front garden of the house to the left of this rural scene.

1913
An unusual picture, eventually traced to the junction of the Stawell and Chedzoy to Sutton Mallet roads, and miles from anywhere. At a time when the levels flooded somewhat more heavily than now, the photographer must have rowed or been rowed some distance, presumably using the pollarded willow trees along the road as his navigational guide!

c. 1924
This card was posted in Stawell on 28th May 1924, but whether the scene depicted is of that village is not so certain. A crowd of well dressed people appear to be gathered in an orchard amongst the beehives, watching something taking place sadly hidden from the camera! Although somewhat of a mystery, the card is pleasing, if for no other reason than as a record of costume of the period.

THE SOMERSET

The Somerset peat beds extending beneath 9000 acres or so of the villages of Ashcott, Burtle, Catcott, Edington, Godney, Meare, Shapwick and Westhay to this day still have not become exhausted, despite years of working. The peat, lying eight to sixteen feet below the surface, has been formed into a raised bog over a period of 4000 years, from a combination of soil types, moss, grasses and vegetation common to the area, activated by the effect on them of differing climatic conditions, such as rainfall and heat. The working and removal of peat was then, and to some extent remains today, an industry in itself, and from this series of pictures it is possible to trace the working from start to finish, as it was at the turn of the century and for at least a couple of decades thereafter.

Cutting the peat took place between March and September and until recent years was performed by hand. Two men would work together and after removal of surface vegetation and using a spade designed for the purpose, would cut the blocks, or 'Mumps' as they were called, before

Turfing in Somerset. "Loading."

they were put on a flat barrow and taken to where they were stacked, a process known as 'hiling', and where the mumps dried out. When partly dried the second process began when each 'mump' was cut in three pieces each about 10" by 8" by 8". These smaller pieces were then moved again and gathered into heaps or 'Ruckles', being circular, beehive-shape constructions about five feet in diameter and around six foot high, facilitating a full circulation of the air and completing the drying-out process over a period upwards of a year. Whilst it was man's work to cut and hile, the women and children stacked the 'ruckles' and from time to time turned over the mumps to ensure even drying. The cutters and hilers at around the time of these pictures were earning 15 shillings for a full day's work, the women stackers only taking home 30 shillings for a full week.

It is recorded that during 1919 as much as 4,500 tons of peat left Shapwick station for destinations nationwide, in the main for domestic fuel requirements.

3825 5

Turfing in Somerset. "Selling ½d worth".

3825. 6 Turfing in Somerset "Turf Worker's Cottage."

THURLOXTON

c. 1910
Bond's Green Dragon Inn, now Ye Olde Dragon, faced with mock tudor beams, and still providing the same vital service of ales, beers and spirits, as well as cream teas, pub food, meals and Sunday roasts. This particular postcard was sent as a Christmas greeting by the licensee Samuel Bond and his wife Tilly to relatives at Cross Keys Inn, Norton, Taunton.

c. 1908
Just down the road from Bond's Green Dragon Inn and en route to Broomfield stands number 63, formerly the post office. Fortunately the character of Thurloxton was protected when the A 38 was diverted to bypass the village.

WESTONZOYLAND

c. 1912
Mr. W.A. North standing in the doorway of his home, the board above the door proudly advertising his expertise as saddler and boot repairer, his services as the latter undoubtedly in great demand, given the size and population of the village.

1927

On Wednesday 6th July 1927 over 1000 people in procession made their way from St. Mary's Church to Sedgemoor to witness the planting of two trees in commemoration of the last battle on English soil. Miss Elizabeth Winter of Chedzoy for some time had led the campaign and fund-raising for a permanent memorial on the historic battlefield. In the corner of the field called 'Graveyard', the spot where the dead were buried in 1685, the two trees were planted by Sir Boyd Dawkins, whose father was a former Vicar of Westonzoyland, and Captain C.B. Greenhill J.P., assisted by Master Dudley Marmaduke Ling of Westonzoyland. Lady Boyd Dawkins presented Mr. Oliver Reed with a family Bible containing the following inscription "Presented to Oliver Reed Esq., Manor Farm, Westonzoyland on July 6th 1927 for his gift to the nation in giving land in Graveyard, Sedgemoor to allow a memorial stone to be erected and trees to be planted to the memory of those who fell in the battle of Sedgemoor, July 6th 1685."

Just over a year later, on 26th July 1928, a memorial stone of Cornish granite, designed and erected by Mr. Clifford Hawkes of Bristol Road, Bridgwater, was unveiled by Miss Annie Cole of Bridgwater as The Last Post was played by buglers of the 5th battalion of the Somerset Light Infantry. A minute's silence in honour of the fallen soldiers was followed by the placing of flower bouquets on the stone base by children from the surrounding villages. The stone, erected midway between the two trees planted the year before, bears the inscription "To the Glory of God and in memory of all those who doing the right as they gave it fell in the battle of Sedgemoor 6th July 1685 and lie buried in this field or who for their share in the fight suffered death punishment or transportation pro patria".

Both of these events included speeches by notable personages, hymn singing and prayers, all widely reported in the days that followed. Of particular interest was the telegram sent by Miss Winter to the King and Queen shortly before the tree planting ceremony with a reply the following day "The King and Queen sincerely thank all those assembled to commemorate the battle of Sedgemoor for their good wishes on the anniversary of their Majesties wedding day". One wonders about the whereabouts today of that telegram and hopes it has been preserved. As another interesting aside, a group from the Bridgwater Pageant of June 1927 in which it had portrayed a scene from the battle, took part in the tree-planting ceremony, using rooms in the Three Greyhounds Hotel to don military costume, itself a scene from the past, for it was in that same hotel that the Royalist troops were quartered in 1685.

c. 1915
The corner of Main Road and Fore Street where Mr. John Denman provided the villagers with their needs for over thirty years. Mr. Denman was first listed as a grocer in 1895 and was still selling from the same premises in 1923. The gas lamp on the corner was erected in March 1900 on the same day that the news of the relief of Ladysmith reached the village, apparently of some significance to those who recorded the event!

1911
A picture for local history books, showing some of the village children on June 22nd, just after they had received commemorative Coronation medals from the Reverand C.M. Rodgers. At 11a.m. that day a procession of flag-waving children, led by Mr. G. Heard and, on horseback, Mr. W. Stacey of the West Somerset Yeomanry set of from the school to St. Mary's Church, to the accompaniment of the Ashcott brass band. After a free luncheon in a marquee erected by Mr. J. Lockyer of Bridgwater in the grounds of Court House, each child was presented with a Coronation mug by Mr. Moorhead. There followed sorts events which attracted a very large entry, Mrs Moorhead presenting the prizes to the winners, including Mr. B. Thyer-the 1 mile cycle race, Miss A. Bown-ladies 1/2 mile cycle race, Mr. G. Heard-pebble race, A. Bourne-boy's race 12-14, Bob Selway-boy's 10-12, B. May-boy's 8-10, B. Bown-boy's 6-8, R. Ridgement-girl's 10-12.
A day to remember!

WALFORD CROSS

c. 1929
The filling station when it was owned by J.T. and P.B. Lightfoot and provided not only fuel for passing motor vehicles, but also facilities for the relief of drivers and passengers, proudly advertising its toilets, delicately referred to as 'Cloak Rooms'. The bus shown here en route for Taunton was a Leyland Lion, one of the fleet operated by Western National.

c. 1943
The 'Prince of Wales', a magnificent Burrell steam engine, on its way from Taunton to Bridgwater, here seen taking on water at Walford Lodge. These old showmen's engines, once kings of the road, are now of great attraction at steam rallies.

WOOLAVINGTON

c. 1910
The Church of the Blessed Virgin Mary on Lower Road and towards the junction with Causeway. The house to the right on the corner of Tapps Lane is now called The Old Post Office, which indicates its former service to the community.

c. 1910
Another scene of Lower Road, this time looking west. Number 4, Causeway Farmhouse, helpfully has inscribed over the doorway "T.H. 1743" revealing the year it was built and perhaps the initials of the first owner or builder.

c. 1910
A very clear photographic postcard of Walton Windmill before its conversion in 1926 to a private residence. Records show that a post mill stood on this site on the south side of Walton Hill as far back as 1342, although this windmill was not built until 1790 and rebuilt seven years later. The last miller was Charles Phillips, who operated it until the late 1890's, but what happened between then and 1926 is not clear.

Standing in isolation high up on the hill, this windmill is an appropriate sight with which to bring this book to a close, since from its vantage point on a clear day and with perfect eye one can survey the scenery around 'Bridgwater and the Villages'; their bygone days brought alive in the postcards between these pages.

SELECTIVE INDEX